S0-ADQ-439

Gitolite Essentials

Leverage powerful branch and user access control with Git for your own private collaborative repositories

Sitaram Chamarty

PACKT open source *
PUBLISHING community experience distilled
BIRMINGHAM - MUMBAI

Gitolite Essentials

Copyright © 2014 Packt Publishing

All rights reserved. No part of this book may be reproduced, stored in a retrieval system, or transmitted in any form or by any means, without the prior written permission of the publisher, except in the case of brief quotations embedded in critical articles or reviews.

Every effort has been made in the preparation of this book to ensure the accuracy of the information presented. However, the information contained in this book is sold without warranty, either express or implied. Neither the author, nor Packt Publishing, and its dealers and distributors will be held liable for any damages caused or alleged to be caused directly or indirectly by this book.

Packt Publishing has endeavored to provide trademark information about all of the companies and products mentioned in this book by the appropriate use of capitals. However, Packt Publishing cannot guarantee the accuracy of this information.

First published: April 2014

Production Reference: 1040414

Published by Packt Publishing Ltd.
Livery Place
35 Livery Street
Birmingham B3 2PB, UK.

ISBN 978-1-78328-237-1

www.packtpub.com

Cover Image by Mohamed Raoof (raoofpmajeed@gmail.com)

Credits

Authors
Sitaram Chamarty

Reviewers
Javier Domingo Cansino
milki
Vinh Quốc Nguyễn
Hiren Patel
Giovanni Toraldo

Acquisition Editors
Owen Roberts
Erol Staveley

Content Development Editor
Poonam Jain

Technical Editor
Manal Pednekar

Copy Editors
Roshni Banerjee
Gladson Monteiro

Project Coordinator
Jomin Varghese

Proofreader
Ameesha Green

Indexer
Hemangini Bari

Graphics
Ronak Dhruv
Yuvraj Mannari

Production Coordinator
Kyle Albuquerque

Cover Work
Kyle Albuquerque

About the Author

Sitaram Chamarty has been in the software industry for a number of years. He is a Linux and open source evangelist who has sometimes been called an "open source bigot", which he takes as a compliment. He loves Perl enough to believe, or at least insist, that xkcd 224 is actual fact.

His day job is with Tata Consultancy Services, and he lives and works in Hyderabad, India. His job does not explicitly include evangelizing open source in general and Git in particular, but he pretends it does. He has significant past experience in language conversion and tools, as well as in data warehousing.

He has a postgraduate degree in Computer Science from the Indian Statistical Institute, Kolkata, India.

Acknowledgments

Acknowledgments for this book must necessarily also include acknowledgments for the success and popularity of Gitolite itself, because without that, this book would not exist.

Most of Gitolite's power features were born from users asking for them, or presenting their problems in a way that made me think about how Gitolite could help. In particular, I would like to thank Jesse Keating (Fedora), Jeff Mitchell (KDE), John "Warthog9" Hawley (`kernel.org`), and Prof. Hiren Patel (University of Waterloo), for many such ideas as well as hours spent brainstorming about features.

The Git and Gitolite communities on IRC channels #git and #gitolite, which are part of freenode, are comprised of a fantastic bunch of people. They've certainly helped more people with Gitolite than I have; Gitolite's popularity is almost entirely because of folks such as "milki", "bremner" (Prof. David Bremner), "ojacobson" (Owen Jacobson), "EugeneKay" (Eugene E. Kashpureff Jr), and many others.

I would like to thank my supervisor and my colleagues at TCS for their encouragement, not just in writing this book but with my involvement in Gitolite itself. In particular, Gitolite's mirroring feature would not have been what it is without some of their input and use cases.

I would also like to thank my reviewers milki, Javier Domingo Cansino, and Hiren Patel for their tireless efforts at fixing up my writing and making me see reason in several instances. Any errors that remain are, of course, entirely mine.

Finally, I would like to thank my wife and kids for putting up with me while writing the book, especially my wife for keeping the chapter schedule on the fridge door!

About the Reviewers

Javier Domingo Cansino got started in University with the open source community and got specialized in Git source code management and several Linux tools.

Through his Git knowledge, which he gained by working on Gitolite projects from the very beginning, he helps people to have a correct Gitolite installation together with appropriate workflows.

With several developments during his career in various languages, and knowledge on kernel networking design, now he is developing in C and Python. He can be found over the Internet under the nickname "txomon".

milki is a recent graduate from the University of California, Berkeley, and now works as a software engineer at Yelp, Inc. in San Francisco, California. During his university years, milki mastered Git and FreeBSD as a software developer and a system administrator. milki contributes to the open source project Dulwich, which is a pure python implementation of the Git file formats and protocol. milki also maintains the FreeBSD port of Gitolite, ensuring Gitolite remains free of Linux-specific code. On freenode IRC, milki can be found in #git, #gitolite, and #github, providing users with general advice from Git basics and troubleshooting to best practices and Git internals.

Hiren Patel is an assistant professor in the Electrical and Computer Engineering department at the University of Waterloo, Canada. His research interests are in embedded software and hardware systems. This includes models of computation, real-time systems, computer architecture, and system-level design methodologies.

Giovanni Toraldo is an open source enthusiast with in-depth knowledge about system administration, cloud computing, and web application development. He currently works as a lead developer for ClouDesire.

In the past, he wrote *OpenNebula 3 Cloud Computing* and reviewed *Mastering Redmine* for Packt Publishing.

www.PacktPub.com

Support files, eBooks, discount offers and more

You might want to visit www.PacktPub.com for support files and downloads related to your book.

Did you know that Packt offers eBook versions of every book published, with PDF and ePub files available? You can upgrade to the eBook version at www.PacktPub.com and as a print book customer, you are entitled to a discount on the eBook copy. Get in touch with us at service@packtpub.com for more details.

At www.PacktPub.com, you can also read a collection of free technical articles, sign up for a range of free newsletters and receive exclusive discounts and offers on Packt books and eBooks.

http://PacktLib.PacktPub.com

Do you need instant solutions to your IT questions? PacktLib is Packt's online digital book library. Here, you can access, read and search across Packt's entire library of books.

Why Subscribe?

- Fully searchable across every book published by Packt
- Copy and paste, print and bookmark content
- On demand and accessible via web browser

Free Access for Packt account holders

If you have an account with Packt at www.PacktPub.com, you can use this to access PacktLib today and view nine entirely free books. Simply use your login credentials for immediate access.

Table of Contents

Preface

Gitolite is a very popular tool for fine-grained access control of Git repository servers. It's fast, unobtrusive, and has a very small footprint, yet it provides several features that make an administrator's life much easier.

This book helps you get up to speed with Gitolite. It is easy to read and flows smoothly all the way from the basic installation process to advanced features such as mirroring. In particular, the more powerful and complex features are built up gradually to help you understand it more intuitively. Anyone who is using or considering using Gitolite should benefit from this book.

What this book covers

Chapter 1, Getting Started with Gitolite, shows you why Gitolite is useful along with some examples of basic access control rules as well as some advanced features. It also shows you how to create a test instance of Gitolite to help you try it out safely.

Chapter 2, Installing Gitolite, talks about installing Gitolite and basic administration tasks such as adding a new user and creating a new repository.

Chapter 3, Your Users and Gitolite, discusses how users see a Gitolite-managed system and what they need to know to start using it. It also has useful information on finding and fixing problems with ssh keys.

Chapter 4, Adding and Removing Users, goes into more detail on user management and what happens behind the scenes when you add a user. Special case situations such as users with multiple keys or users who need a full shell command line are discussed.

Chapter 5, Managing Repositories, talks about adding new repositories as well as bringing existing repositories into Gitolite control.

Chapter 6, Getting Started with Access Control, shows most of Gitolite's basic access control features, including various types of access rules and the configuration file syntax.

Chapter 7, Advanced Access Control and Configuration, goes into advanced features such as personal branches, setting Git config variables, and Gitolite options. It also discusses how Gitolite can be made to affect the operation of gitweb and git-daemon.

Chapter 8, Allowing Users to Create Repos, talks about a feature that is probably one of Gitolite's most popular and important features. It discusses how to allow users to create their own repositories, how the access rules work, and what the creator of a repository can do to allow others to access it.

Chapter 9, Customizing Gitolite, shows how administrators can add unique features to their site using Gitolite's customization capabilities, such as commands and triggers.

Chapter 10, Understanding VREFs, talks about Gitolite's ability to use arbitrary factors to make the allow/reject decision when a user pushes to a repository, with only a few lines of code to be written in most cases.

Chapter 11, Mirroring, explores a Gitolite feature that is very useful in large multisite setups that have developers in many locations around the world working on common projects. Gitolite mirroring is very flexible, and this chapter will set you on your way to make the best use of it.

What you need for this book

You will need a Unix system with a POSIX compatible "sh", Git Version 1.7.8 or later, and Perl 5.8.8 or later. You will also need the Openssh server (or a compatible ssh server).

Who this book is for

This book is ideal for anyone who is looking to install and use Gitolite. People who are already using it and would like to go beyond the basics and understand its more powerful features will also find a lot of useful information and insights.

Conventions

In this book, you will find a number of styles of text that distinguish between different kinds of information. Here are some examples of these styles, and an explanation of their meaning.

Code words in text, database table names, folder names, filenames, file extensions, pathnames, dummy URLs, user input, and Twitter handles are shown as follows: "One way to convert a non-bare repository to a bare repository is to clone it using the --bare option."

Any command-line input or output is written as follows:

```
repo    gitolite-admin
    RW+    =    adam
repo    testing
    RW+    =    @all
```

New terms and **important words** are shown in bold. Words that you see on the screen, in menus or dialog boxes for example, appear in the text like this: "Clicking on the **Next** button moves you to the next screen."

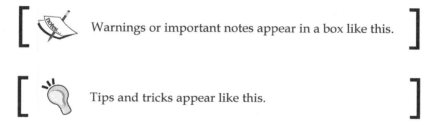

> Warnings or important notes appear in a box like this.

> Tips and tricks appear like this.

Reader feedback

Feedback from our readers is always welcome. Let us know what you think about this book—what you liked or may have disliked. Reader feedback is important for us to develop titles that you really get the most out of.

To send us general feedback, simply send an e-mail to feedback@packtpub.com, and mention the book title via the subject of your message.

If there is a topic that you have expertise in and you are interested in either writing or contributing to a book, see our author guide on www.packtpub.com/authors.

Customer support

Now that you are the proud owner of a Packt book, we have a number of things to help you to get the most from your purchase.

Errata

Although we have taken every care to ensure the accuracy of our content, mistakes do happen. If you find a mistake in one of our books—maybe a mistake in the text or the code—we would be grateful if you would report this to us. By doing so, you can save other readers from frustration and help us improve subsequent versions of this book. If you find any errata, please report them by visiting http://www.packtpub. com/submit-errata, selecting your book, clicking on the **errata submission form** link, and entering the details of your errata. Once your errata are verified, your submission will be accepted and the errata will be uploaded on our website, or added to any list of existing errata, under the Errata section of that title. Any existing errata can be viewed by selecting your title from http://www.packtpub.com/support.

Piracy

Piracy of copyright material on the Internet is an ongoing problem across all media. At Packt, we take the protection of our copyright and licenses very seriously. If you come across any illegal copies of our works, in any form, on the Internet, please provide us with the location address or website name immediately so that we can pursue a remedy.

Please contact us at copyright@packtpub.com with a link to the suspected pirated material.

We appreciate your help in protecting our authors, and our ability to bring you valuable content.

Questions

You can contact us at questions@packtpub.com if you are having a problem with any aspect of the book, and we will do our best to address it.

1
Getting Started with Gitolite

Git is one of the most popular version control systems currently available, and several thousands of projects, new and old, have started using it in the past few years. You might have also used it, and shortly after, realized that Git does not do much for Access Control by itself. You need an access control system that is simple and quick to install and get running, yet flexible and powerful enough for your future needs.

This chapter will describe what Gitolite is, and why you might need it. It shows a few examples of the basic features, and also shows you how you can try out Gitolite safely. It assumes that you have some basic knowledge of Git, and have used Git both locally and with a remote repository.

Common Access Control needs

Git server administrators face a bit of a challenge. The high uptake rate of Git means that there are thousands of developers who are not really familiar with Git, and who therefore may be running Git commands that cause irreversible or highly disruptive changes to the Git repository. Furthermore, Git itself does not help much with this; whatever access controls it has, apply to the entire repository, and cannot be made more fine-grained.

For instance, the master branch in most projects represents the most stable code. Yet, a junior developer can easily run a command such as `git push origin +master`, (which pushes the developer's local branch onto the server) and thus overwrite weeks or months of hardwork by the rest of the team. People with deeper Git expertise can probably recover the lost commits, but it would certainly take time and effort.

Worse, Git's command syntax sometimes makes it worse. For example, the command to delete the master branch is only slightly different from a normal push, that is, `git push origin :master` (notice the extra colon?).

The most common need, therefore, is to prevent these kinds of accidents: overwriting (or rewinding) one or more commits, and deleting a branch or a tag.

Git itself does provide some measure of protection. You can set the config items `receive.denyDeletes` and `receive.denyNonFastForwards` to `true`. Unfortunately, this is a bit of a blunt instrument—now no one can delete or rewind *any* branch!

In larger setups with several repositories and several developers, you may also be concerned about allowing everyone to read all repositories. Or it may be that some roles (such as a test engineer) should not need to write to the repository; read-only access is sufficient. Up to a certain point, this problem can be solved with Unix permissions and user/group permissions applied judiciously. Perhaps even POSIX ACLs can be used if you're comfortable with that sort of thing.

However, using POSIX ACLs and user/group permissions has several disadvantages:

- Each Git user needs a corresponding Unix user ID on the server.
- Managing access rights can only be done by using the `usermod` and `setfacl` commands.
- Checking the current set of permissions is not straightforward. You will need to run multiple commands and correlate their output manually.
- Auditing changes in permissions over time is impossible because no history is kept by the system.

These disadvantages require a lot of effort to manage even a few repositories and users, and even a modestly sized setup would quickly become unmanageable.

Access Control example with Gitolite

We will see how simple Access Control can be with Gitolite. First, here's an example where the junior developers (let's call them Alice and Bob here) should be prevented from rewinding or deleting any branches, while the senior developers (Carol and David) are allowed to do so:

 We will see this in more detail in later chapters, but Gitolite uses a plain text file to specify the configuration, and these access rules are placed in that file.

```
repo foo
    RW    =  alice bob
    RW+   =  carol david
```

You probably guessed that the RW stands for read and write. The + in the second rule stands for *force*, just as it does in the push command, and allows you to rewind or delete a branch.

Now, suppose we want the junior developers to have some specific set of branches that they should be allowed to rewind or delete, a sort of "sandbox", if you will. The following command will help you to implement that:

```
RW+  sandbox/  =  alice bob
```

Alice and Bob can now push, rewind, or delete any branches whose names start with sandbox/.

Access Control at the repository level is even easier, and you may even have guessed what that looks like:

```
repo foo
    RW+     =   alice
    R       =   bob


repo bar
    RW+     =   bob
    R       =   alice


repo baz
    RW+     =   carol
    R       =   alice bob
```

As you can see, you have three users with different access permissions for each of the three repositories. Doing this using the file systems' permissions mechanisms or POSIX ACLs would be doable, but quite cumbersome to set up and to audit/review.

Sampling of Gitolite's power features

The access control examples show the most commonly used feature of Gitolite, the repository and branch level access control, but of course Gitolite has many more features. In this section, we will briefly look at a few of them while noting that there are many more waiting in the wings for you to find as you read this book.

Creating groups

Gitolite allows you to create groups of users or repositories for convenience. Think back to Alice and Bob, our junior developers. Let's say you had several rules that Alice and Bob needed to be mentioned in. Clearly, this is too cumbersome; every time a new developer joined the team, you'd have to change all the rules to add him or her.

Gitolite lets you do this by using the following command:

```
@junior-devs    =  alice bob
```

Later, it lets you do this by using the following command:

```
repo foo
  RW                   =  @junior-devs
  RW+                  =  carol david
  RW+  sandbox/        =  @junior-devs
```

This allows you to add the junior developer in just one place at the top of the configuration file instead of potentially several places all over. More importantly, from the administrator's point of view, it serves as excellent documentation for the rules themselves; isn't it easier to reason about the rules when a descriptive group name is used rather than actual usernames?

Personal branches

Gitolite allows the administrator to give each developer a unique set of branches, called personal branches, that only he or she can create, push, or delete. This is a very convenient way to allow quick backups of work-in-progress branches, or share code for preliminary review.

We saw how the sandbox area was defined:

```
  RW+  sandbox/  =  alice bob
```

However, this does nothing to prevent one junior developer from accidentally wiping out another's branches. For example, Alice could delete a branch called sandbox/bob/work that Bob may have pushed. You can use the special word USER as a directory name to solve this problem:

```
  RW+  sandbox/USER/  =  alice bob
```

This works as if you had specified each user individually, like this:

```
  RW+  sandbox/alice/  =  alice
  RW+  sandbox/bob/     =  bob
```

Now, the set of branches that Alice is allowed to push is limited to those starting with `sandbox/alice/`, and she can no longer push or delete a branch called, say, `sandbox/bob/work`.

Personal repositories

With Gitolite, the administrator can choose to let the user create their own repositories, in addition to the ones that the administrator themselves creates. For this example, ignore the syntax, which will be explained in a much later chapter, but just focus on the functionality now:

```
repo dev/CREATOR/[a-z].*
    C       =   @staff
    RW+     =   CREATOR
```

This allows members of the `@staff` group to create repositories whose names match the pattern supplied, which just means `dev/<username>/<anything starting with a lowercase alphabetic character>`. For example, a user called `alice` will be able to create repositories such as `dev/alice/foo` and `dev/alice/bar`.

Gitolite and the Git control flow

Conceptually, Gitolite is a very simple program. To see how it controls access to a Git repository, let us first look at how control flows from the client to the server in a normal git operation (say `git fetch`) when using plain `ssh`:

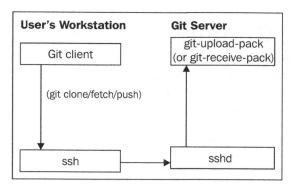

When the user executes a **git clone**, **fetch**, or **push**, the **Git client** invokes `ssh`, passing it a command (either `git-upload-pack` or `git-receive-pack`, depending on whether the user is reading or writing). The local ssh client passes this to the server, and assuming authentication succeeds, that command gets executed on the server.

With Gitolite installed, the `ssh` daemon does not invoke the `git-upload-pack` or `git-receive-pack` directly. Instead, it calls a program called `gitolite-shell`, which changes the control flow as follows:

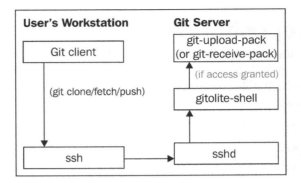

First, notice that nothing changes on the **Git client** side in any way; the changes are only on the server side. In fact, unless an access violation happens and an error message needs to be sent to the user, the user may not even *know* that Gitolite is installed!

Second, notice the red link from Gitolite's shell program to the `git-upload-pack` program. This call does not happen if Gitolite determines that the user does not have the appropriate access to the repo concerned. This access check happens for both read (that is, `git fetch` and `git clone` commands) and write (`git push`) operations; although for writes, there are more checks that happen later.

Trying out Gitolite

It's very easy to try out Gitolite in a safe environment without affecting anything else in the system in any permanent manner. Gitolite has a fairly complete set of test scripts, and the officially supported method of trying out Gitolite simply uses a couple of these test scripts to automatically install and set up Gitolite.

At the end of this process, you will have a version of Gitolite all set up and ready to use. You will also have an "admin" user, and six "normal" users, using which you can try out most of the features of Gitolite (with the exception of some advanced features such as mirroring).

Preparing for the setup

You will need the following in order to try out Gitolite:

- A Unix (Linux, BSD, HP-UX, AIX, Solaris, and so on) server
- Git version 1.7.1 or later installed on the server
- Perl 5.8.8 or later version installed on the server
- An OpenSSH-compatible SSH daemon installed and running on the server
- Root access to the server in order to create a new throw away user to do the testing in

At the time of writing this book, Git 1.7.1 is over three years old, and Perl 5.8.8 is quite a bit older than that, so almost any recent Linux or BSD system should work fine.

Installing and setting up a test instance

With the prerequisites at hand, here's how you would get yourself a `test` instance of Gitolite to try out:

1. Log in as root (using whatever commands your OS/distro requires to do that) and create a new throw away user. You can call this anything you want, but we will use the name `gitolite-test` here. *Please do not use an existing user for this!*
2. Log in as the `gitolite-test` user.
3. Get the Gitolite sources from the official repository, `git clone git://github.com/gitolite/gitolite`.

   You can get this from any other clone of the gitolite sources if your server cannot directly access the internet. Just substitute the URL you have in the preceding `clone` command.

4. Switch to the directory that was just cloned using the following command:
   `cd gitolite`

5. Install and set up Gitolite in test mode using the following command:
   `env GITOLITE_TEST=y prove t/ssh*`

6. Go back to the HOME directory:

   `cd`

This will churn through two of the test scripts. You will see a warning about an `authorized_keys` file being created, which you can ignore, and finally a message saying `All tests successful`, with some statistics on the test run.

At the end of that process, you should have the following: one "admin" user (called `admin`) and six normal users (named `u1` through `u6`). These users are simulated using an `ssh` feature. If you are familiar with `ssh`, you can look in `~/.ssh/config` to see how this is done.

Playing with Gitolite

You can now use the test setup of gitolite from the previous section. Here's a sample set of commands with notes to start you off:

Clone the special `gitolite-admin` repository:

```
$ git clone admin:gitolite-admin
Cloning into 'gitolite-admin'...
remote: Counting objects: 8, done.
remote: Compressing objects: 100% (4/4), done.
remote: Total 8 (delta 1), reused 0 (delta 0)
Receiving objects: 100% (8/8), done.
Resolving deltas: 100% (1/1), done.
```

Examine the contents of the clone:

```
$ cd gitolite-admin/
$ ls -a
.  ..  conf  .git
$ ls -a conf
.  ..  gitolite.conf
```

Edit the `conf/gitolite.conf` file and add the following lines, which tell Gitolite to create a new repository called `bar` and allow users `u1` and `u2` all rights to it:

```
repo bar
  RW+  =  u1 u2
```

Save the file, then add the change (`git add`) and commit the file (`git commit`):

```
$ git add conf/gitolite.conf
$ git commit -m 'added repo bar'
[master 1111cee] added repo bar
```

```
  1 file changed, 3 insertions(+)
$ git push
Counting objects: 7, done.
Delta compression using up to 4 threads.
Compressing objects: 100% (2/2), done.
Writing objects: 100% (4/4), 338 bytes | 0 bytes/s, done.
Total 4 (delta 1), reused 0 (delta 0)
remote: Initialized empty Git repository in /home/gitolite-test/
repositories/bar.git/
To admin:gitolite-admin
   f226f28..1111cee  master -> master
```

As you can see, we've just created a new repository called bar. If you look at the output carefully, you might notice, among the familiar output of a git push command, a line saying that an empty Git repository was initialized on the server. This is useful because you don't have to log on to the server to create the repository—Gitolite takes care of it.

Let's look at some access rights. Running ssh against the server and supplying info as the command will show you what repositories you have access to:

```
$ ssh admin info
hello admin, this is gitolite-test@server running gitolite3 v3.5.3.1-6-
g5bdc750 on git 1.8.3.1

  R W  gitolite-admin
  R W  testing
$ ssh u1 info
hello u1, this is gitolite-test@server running gitolite3 v3.5.3.1-6-
g5bdc750 on git 1.8.3.1

  R W  bar
  R W  foo
  R W  testing
$ ssh u3 info
hello u3, this is gitolite-test@server running gitolite3 v3.5.3.1-6-
g5bdc750 on git 1.8.3.1

  R W  foo
  R W  testing
```

The preceding command shows you a list of the repositories you have access to, and for each of them, whether you can read and write to the repository, or you have read-only access.

A note on command and URL syntax

Remember that we are running the Gitolite server, as well as simulating the seven different users, on the same Unix user (which is `gitolite-test`). As a result, you are able to use commands such as `git clone admin:gitolite-admin` and `ssh u1 info`. In a real setup, you will represent yourself, and the server will be elsewhere. The commands will be of the form `git clone gitolite-test@server:gitolite-admin` and `ssh gitolite-test@server info`.

Summary

In this chapter, we learned why Gitolite is useful, saw an example of access control rules, and got a glimpse of some of its features. We also learned the basic ideas behind Gitolite, and created a test instance of Gitolite in order to try it out safely.

In the next chapter, we will install Gitolite properly and learn the basics of administering Gitolite.

2
Installing Gitolite

The previous chapter showed you how to set up what we might call a **sandbox** installation of Gitolite, suitable for experimenting with the software and getting comfortable with it. We did that using a script that hid most of the details of the install process so that you could *get to the good stuff*.

In this chapter, we will actually perform a proper install of Gitolite. We will start with the prerequisites on the server and move on to the actual install steps. By the end of this chapter, you should have a working installation of Gitolite that is ready to support users and serve up repositories to them securely, enforcing access restrictions as you specify them.

Gitolite users and the hosting user

Gitolite provides access to several Gitolite users, using only one actual user ID on the server. Before we start installing and setting up Gitolite, it's useful to have some knowledge of what is actually going on behind the scenes and how this is achieved.

Gitolite uses one Unix user called the **hosting user** to provide repository access to many Gitolite users. The hosting user can be any valid user on the system, though by convention it is either git or gitolite. This is the only user ID that is used by Gitolite on the server, and it is within the home directory of this user that Gitolite places its files, its own configuration, as well as the repositories it manages.

Gitolite can support thousands of Gitolite users on one server. These users are not *real* users as far as the server operating system is concerned, and they do not get access to the shell command line on the server. A Gitolite user does, however, get access to some of the repositories on the server so that they can run Git commands against them.

Distinguishing users from each other

Gitolite uses ssh to authenticate its users. However, while ssh normally allows authentication using either a password or an ssh key pair, Gitolite requires that a key pair be used for authentication; passwords are not accepted.

Each Gitolite user has an ssh key pair on their desktop or laptop. A key pair consists of two files, typically called id_rsa (the private key), and id_rsa.pub (the public key).

The public key file contains a single, very long line of text; here's a shortened example:

```
ssh-rsa AAAAB3NzaC1[...]LBkU1XGGPnX adam@lab1.example.com
```

The key is actually too long to print here, so we removed about 350 characters from the middle, replacing them with ellipsis, but this should still give you a good idea of what it looks like.

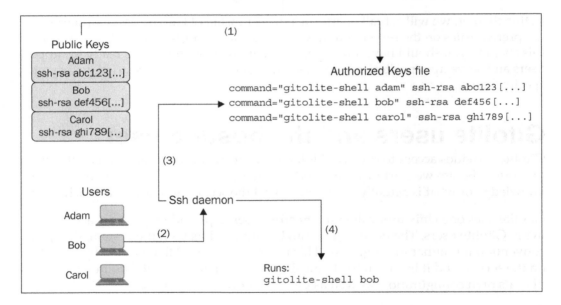

The preceding figure illustrates the sequence of events that happens when a user connects to a Gitolite server to access a Git repository, and how this sequence is enabled. First, each user sends their public key to the Gitolite administrator. When the Gitolite administrator adds these users to Gitolite, Gitolite adds the keys to a file called `.ssh/authorized_keys` in the home directory of the hosting user. It then prefixes to the beginning of each line a string that looks somewhat like the following line (for the user Adam) and similarly for other users:

```
command="/home/gitolite/bin/gitolite-shell adam",[...] ssh-rsa [...]
```

This first step is what enables the access control. It is a one-time action, and needs to be repeated only when the administrator adds or removes users. Notice the `command` option, containing a program name (`gitolite-shell` using its full path), and its argument (the username, `adam` in this example) — this will be relevant a bit later.

The second step shows what happens when, say, Bob tries to connect to the server. Bob runs the ssh command, whether directly or via his local git client, in the form of a clone, fetch, or push command. The ssh daemon on the server handles the connection attempt. Bob's ssh client will offer a public key, and the ssh daemon will go looking for it in the authorized keys file, finding it eventually. In our example, it finds a match on the second line.

Next, the ssh daemon notices the command option on the matched line in the authorized keys file. This tells the ssh daemon that, instead of running the program that the client asked for, it should instead run the command mentioned in that option, including any arguments supplied. This means the `gitolite-shell` program is executed with the Gitolite username (in our example, Bob) as the first argument. This is how the `gitolite-shell` program knows who is connecting.

> For those who are wondering what happened to the original command that the git client actually wanted, the ssh daemon stores it in an environment variable called `SSH_ORIGINAL_COMMAND` and passes it to the `gitolite-shell` program, which knows what to do with it.

Preparing the server

Gitolite can be installed on any Unix server. This includes Linux, any of the BSDs, and the legacy Unix servers such as AIX and HP-UX. With that said, here are the requirements:

- A Unix system with a POSIX-compatible sh (shell)
- Git Version 1.7.1 or higher

- Perl 5.8.8 or higher
- OpenSSH 5.0 or higher
- A dedicated Unix user as the hosting user described previously, whose home directory must be on a filesystem that supports symlinks, and allows executables (that is, it is not mounted with the `noexec` mount flag)

Ideally, you should use a brand new user ID that has no existing files or directories, except for whatever a newly created user gets (such as the bashrc or similar files). This will ensure that any leftover files don't interfere.

Getting the Gitolite source

The next step is to obtain the Gitolite source code. The simplest way to do this, if your server can connect to the Internet, is to run `git clone git://github.com/sitaramc/gitolite`.

If you do not have direct access to the Internet, simply use some other machine in between. For example, you could run the previous command on a server that can connect to the Internet. From that intermediate server, you can zip the entire Gitolite repository, bring it over to the Gitolite server, and unzip it.

Installing the code

The first step is to put the source code where you want it to go. Gitolite is designed in a way that it doesn't require root (except to create the hosting user), so you can (and usually should) put it somewhere within the home directory of the Gitolite hosting user. For our discussion, we will pick `$HOME/bin`, because this is usually included in the user's PATH setting.

Log in as the hosting user, and run the following commands:

```
cd $HOME
mkdir -p $HOME/bin
gitolite/install --to $HOME/bin
```

For people who are familiar with commands such as `make prefix=/usr/local install`, this is conceptually not very different.

Setting up Gitolite

Now that the code is in the right place, we need to set it up. Setting it up involves adding an ssh public key for the main administrator of the Gitolite installation. In this book, we will assume the administrator's name is Adam, thus his Gitolite username will be `adam`, but as you follow along, please substitute your own name wherever you see references to Adam or `adam`.

Ssh is a powerful and complex tool. To make things simpler in this chapter, we will describe a set of steps that would surely work, along with suitable assumptions and constraints. These constraints are not absolutely necessary, but they do serve to simplify our procedure, as well as remove potential troublespots. If you're very familiar with SSH, you will probably be able to get around them quite easily.

Creating an ssh key pair

The administrator needs to first create an ssh key pair for themselves at their main workstation. In many cases, there may already be an ssh key pair, possibly generated for some other purpose. You should look in `$HOME/.ssh` for a pair of files called `id_rsa` and `id_rsa.pub`. If you don't find any such files, you can generate a key pair by running the `ssh-keygen` command.

Ideally, you will choose a strong passphrase to protect your private key when generating your ssh key pair. To use it without having to constantly type the passphrase, you will then use the `ssh-agent` command or any of its derivatives, such as the keychain package. However, these nuances are out of the scope of this book.

Similarly, if you had previously created a non-default key type (that is, something other than RSA for ssh protocol 2, which is the default), then it is assumed that you know what you are doing. Gitolite should work fine with DSA and ECDSA key pairs, but will probably not work with RSA protocol 1 keys.

Running the setup command

Now that you have your key pair at your workstation, you will need to get the public key (and *only* the public key!) over to the Gitolite hosting user's home directory on the server. One way to do this is to use the `scp` command, as in `scp .ssh/id_rsa.pub git@host:adam.pub`. You can use any other method available to you, for example rsync, or sftp, or even a USB stick. It doesn't matter how you do it as long as the file gets there and is renamed as `adam.pub`.

A word of warning for ssh experts: do not be tempted to automatically add this key to the Gitolite hosting user's authorized keys file using a command such as `ssh-copy-id`.

Once you have copied the file, you are ready to run the actual setup command, which is as follows:

```
gitolite setup -pk adam.pub
```

This command should produce an output similar to the following:

```
Initialized empty Git repository in /home/gitolite-test/repositories/
gitolite-admin.git/
```

```
Initialized empty Git repository in /home/gitolite-test/repositories/
testing.git/
```

```
WARNING: /home/gitolite-test/.ssh/authorized_keys missing; creating a new
one
```

You can ignore the warning about the authorized keys file being created — this is quite normal for the first time you do this. And with that, your Gitolite installation and setup are all done.

Checking over your new Gitolite server

Very few Gitolite administration tasks require logging on to the server and using the command line. Most of the day-to-day maintenance tasks (especially adding users and repositories) are done by making changes to a special repository called `gitolite-admin`, and pushing those changes to the server; that is, the administrator must perform the following:

1. Clone the `gitolite-admin` repository.
2. Add some files or make changes to existing files.
3. Commit the changes.
4. Push them to the server (an administrator is someone who is allowed to push to the `gitolite-admin` repo). When the push completes, Gitolite on the server side invokes specific scripts to effect the changes requested.

You should be able to clone the gitolite-admin repository from your workstation by running `git clone git@server:gitolite-admin`. Git will use ssh to connect to the "git" user on the "server". By default, it will look at your `$HOME/.ssh` directory, find your ssh key pair, and offer the public key to the server to authenticate you. After that, things proceed pretty much as described in the earlier section on distinguishing users from each other, and Gitolite gives you access to the repository.

You should now see the usual message from a successful `git clone` operation, and you can enter `cd gitolite-admin` to see what came in:

```
$ cd gitolite-admin
$ ls -a
.   ..   conf   .git   keydir
$ ls -a conf keydir
conf:
.   ..   gitolite.conf

keydir:
.   ..   adam.pub
```

You can see where the public keys are stored. Note that Gitolite's notion of what your Gitolite username is, comes solely from the name of the public key file in the `keydir` directory. This is why when you copied the `id_rsa.pub` file from your workstation you copied it as `adam.pub`.

 Ssh experts may note that the comment field inside the public key file is ignored; it would be against the conventional meaning of the word "comment" to use it for anything that causes a behavioral change in a system, despite the number of people on the Internet who appear to think it has a higher purpose.

Adding a user

Although we will cover adding users in detail in a later chapter, you may want to add a beta user right away. Let's say you want to add Bob; here's how you can do this:

1. Get his public key, rename it to `bob.pub`.
2. Copy it to the `keydir` directory you saw above (that is, in your local clone of the `gitolite-admin` repository).
3. Add the file, commit, and push.

Adding a repository

Looking inside the `conf/gitolite.conf` file shows us the following:

```
$ cat conf/gitolite.conf
repo gitolite-admin
    RW+     =     adam


repo testing
    RW+     =     @all
```

To add a new repository, edit this file and add a repo line similar to the ones that were added previously, followed by an access rule line, sticking to the syntax shown previously for now. Save the file, add it, commit the change, and push the commit. You should immediately see the usual response from the remote git for a successful push, but also something like the following:

```
remote: Initialized empty Git repository in /home/gitolite-test/
repositories/t2.git/
```

This indicates that the new repository is ready for use.

Summary

In this chapter, we installed Gitolite, learned about the special `gitolite-admin` repository and its contents, and added a new user and a new repository. In the next chapter, we will talk about what a Gitolite-managed Git repository server will look like to your users and what they can do with it.

3
Your Users and Gitolite

Now that we have a working installation of Gitolite, it's time to talk about how users interact with a Gitolite-managed system, and what they need to know to start using it. This will allow you to get some of your advanced users to start using the system while you continue to learn about Gitolite as we progress. As an administrator, you will be making a lot of decisions in terms of things such as naming conventions for repositories as well as branches, how tight or relaxed the access rules will be, and many more aspects that you will learn going forward. These advanced users could help by giving you feedback or acting as sounding boards for these decisions.

Accessing Git repositories

Before discussing how to access a Gitolite-managed repository, we will first need some background on how Git repositories are normally accessed, that is, when you aren't using Gitolite.

Git servers, SSH, and HTTP

We start by reviewing how a user views a normal Git server. Git repositories use URLs as locators, so when a user clones, fetches from, or pushes to a remote repository, it is done using a suitable URL. Git URLs are not very different from any other URL, and the man page for git-clone has a section on them, so you can see all the syntax variations that you can use.

However, for authenticated remote access, there are really only two protocols that are of interest: SSH and HTTP. Of these, ssh-based access is a lot more common, because it is quick and easy to set up; even on a freshly installed Unix, there's usually no extra configuration required to get it working.

As the main page mentioned previously says an ssh URL has the general form `ssh://[user@]host.xz[:port]/path/to/repo.git`. When you type an URL, such as `ssh://git@server.example.com/repo` to access a remote git repository, you will usually be asked for a password, unless an ssh key pair has already been set up for access to the remote host. Once access has been granted, the ssh daemon runs the appropriate Git command on the remote side to talk to the Git client on the local side.

Accessing Gitolite repositories

With the background from the previous section, we're ready to see how things change when a user goes through Gitolite to access a Git repository.

> This section will contain the basic material that most administrators would need to provide to their users, or to explain to them how to access a Gitolite server. However, depending on your users' familiarity with ssh and related topics, you may have to expand this material with supplementary information, examples, or instructions specific to your site.

SSH key pairs

The most significant change is that password access is no longer possible; users *must* use a key pair and send the public key to the administrator so that they can be added to Gitolite. If this does not happen, Gitolite has no way to recognize the user.

If they don't already have an ssh key pair, they should generate one on their own workstations.

Your users will need to use the `ssh-keygen` command to create the key pair. This creates two files, which are `id_rsa` containing the private key and `id_rsa.pub` containing the public key, if they chose the default options. On a Windows system, the command will respond with the full paths of where the files were created, while on a Unix system they will be in `$HOME/.ssh`.

> Ideally, users should set a passphrase on the private key for security and then use `ssh-agent` for convenience; however, both of these topics are out of the scope of this book. Any ssh-related text or website should have sufficient details, as will the documentation that comes with the OpenSSH package.

They will then send the public key (the file whose name ends in `.pub`) to you, so that you may add them as a user.

Repository naming

The second change is that the name of each repository will be whatever you, as the administrator, have created in the `conf/gitolite.conf` file that we briefly saw in the last section of the previous chapter. Gitolite actually creates all its repositories inside `$HOME/repositories` in the hosting user account, but only you (the administrator) need to know this. As far as the user is concerned, to access a repository that is listed in the conf file as `repo foo`, the URL to use is simply `git@server:foo` (or the longer form `ssh://git@server/foo`).

Also, note that the `.git` at the end of the repository name is optional for Git commands (namely `clone`, `fetch`, `push`, `ls-remote`, and `archive`). Git itself works fine with or without it, so Gitolite does the same in order to be consistent. However, in interactions with Gitolite, such as when running Gitolite commands that refer to repositories, you must use the bare name (without the trailing `.git`), which is the name that Gitolite prints in its error messages or informational output.

Getting information from Gitolite

Once your users have access to Gitolite, they would probably like to see which repositories they can access. The simplest way to do this is to run the `info` command, which is available to all remote users:

```
$ ssh git@server info
hello adam, this is git@server running gitolite3 v3.5.3.1-7-g5f88a09 on
git 1.8.3.1
  R W   gitolite-admin
  R W   t2
  R W   testing
```

This tells you what your Gitolite username is (in this case, `adam`), which repos you have access to, and whether you are allowed to read and write, or only read but not write to the repo. Apart from that, this command also tells you which version of Gitolite and which version of Git is running on the server, which could be useful.

Gitolite commands

The `info` command is not the only command available to your users, of course; there are a few more. As you may have guessed from the preceding part, the general format for running Gitolite commands is simply `ssh git@server command-name command-arguments`, where the arguments are of course optional.

Conveniently, Gitolite also has a command to list all the available commands:

```
$ ssh git@server help
hello adam, this is gitolite3 v3.5.3.1-7-g5f88a09 on git 1.8.3.1

list of remote commands available:

    desc
    help
    info
    perms
    writable
```

As you can see, this gives the remote user the list of commands that they are allowed to run. (Some of these commands can only be explained in later chapters).

Further, if you run this from the Gitolite hosting user command line, as `gitolite help`, you will get a listing of *all* the available commands, and not just the ones that are enabled for remote access.

Getting help for commands

Getting help for a command is easy. Every Gitolite command responds with a help message when called with `-h` as the only argument. For example, the help message for the info command is given as follows:

```
$ ssh git@server info -h

Usage:  gitolite info [-lc] [-ld] [<repo name pattern>]

List all existing repos you can access, as well as repo name patterns you
can
```

```
create repos from (if any).

        '-lc'       lists creators as an additional field at the end.
        '-ld'       lists description as an additional field at the end.


The optional pattern is an unanchored regex that will limit the repos

searched, in both cases.   It might speed up things a little if you have
more

than a few thousand repos.
```

As before, some of these options pertain to features of Gitolite we have not yet encountered, and will become clearer when that material is presented.

Troubleshooting SSH issues

When you start adding your first few users to a system, you may run into some ssh-related issues. This section will discuss the possible issues in brief, and explain how to recognize and fix them.

Authorization, not authentication

First, we need a couple of basic definitions. Authentication is the process of verifying that you are who you claim to be. Authorization is the process of determining what you want to do and deciding whether you're allowed to do it or not. Authorization happens after authentication (the system can only decide what you are allowed to do *after* establishing who you are!).

Gitolite is only concerned with authorization; it does not do authentication. It leaves authentication up to an ssh server or a web server.

 The HTTP mode is out of scope for this book; please consult Gitolite's online documentation to use that mode.

Once the ssh server has authenticated the user, it uses the command option in the ssh authorized keys file ($HOME/.ssh/authorized_keys) to invoke Gitolite and pass it the username. Gitolite then decides whether this user is allowed to access this repository or not.

Duplicate public keys

If the user's public key was already part of the authorized keys file before setting up Gitolite (perhaps to allow him to get a login shell and run Unix commands), the key will appear twice in the authorized keys file — once as is, and once with the command option and other options that Gitolite adds to each public key in the keydir directory.

However, if a key appears twice in the authorized keys file, the ssh server will only look at the first occurrence. At the same time, Gitolite tries very hard to make sure that a key that already had normal access to the server continues to have it, so it will place the Gitolite line, which is more restrictive than the default access, *after* the normal line. This means that users who have shell access to the Gitolite hosting user will not be able to use Gitolite, since the key will not invoke Gitolite. They will need to create and use a different ssh key pair for Gitolite (that is, repository) access. They would then have to manage these two key pairs on their client, perhaps using $HOME/.ssh/config to help. Further explanation of the ssh config file and how it helps you choose which key to use, is out of scope for this book. However, almost any decent book on ssh, as well as the main pages for ssh on your system, should have this information.

Diagnosing public key problems

The best way to diagnose public key problems, such as in the previous section, is to run the sshkeys-lint program that comes with Gitolite. Here is an example where two problems with public keys were intentionally created. The first is that we reused a key that already had shell access, adding it to Gitolite as u2.pub. The second is that we copied the file u5.pub as u6.pub. The output of the sshkeys-lint command after these changes is given as follows:

```
$ gitolite sshkeys-lint
sshkeys-lint: ==== checking authkeys file:
sshkeys-lint: WARNING: authkeys line 5 (user u2) will be ignored by sshd;
same key found on line 1 (shell access)
sshkeys-lint: WARNING: authkeys line 9 (user u6) will be ignored by sshd;
same key found on line 8 (user u5)
sshkeys-lint: ==== checking pubkeys:
sshkeys-lint: admin.pub maps to user admin
sshkeys-lint: u1.pub maps to user u1
sshkeys-lint: u2.pub maps to shell access
sshkeys-lint: u3.pub maps to user u3
```

```
sshkeys-lint: u4.pub maps to user u4
sshkeys-lint: u5.pub maps to user u5
sshkeys-lint: WARNING: u6.pub appears to be a COPY of u5.pub
sshkeys-lint: u6.pub maps to user u5
```

```
3 warnings found
```

As you can see, the command lists potential problems, first in the authorized keys file (`$HOME/.ssh/authorized_keys`), and then among the public keys that Gitolite owns.

SSH best practice

We've now seen how to troubleshoot ssh issues. However, it's better to avoid such problems in the first place, and a good rule of thumb for avoiding them is this: don't give any user shell access to the server. Even you, as the administrator, should log on to some other user ID, run `su - git`, and then provide a password when you need to do anything on the Gitolite hosting user's command-line shell. Let all the keys in the authorized keys file be Gitolite-managed keys unless you are really familiar with ssh. That should eliminate most of the common issues with ssh keys.

Summary

In this chapter, we saw how to add users to your new Gitolite installation, and how to find and fix problems with ssh keys. In the next chapter, we will talk about creating new repositories.

Adding and Removing Users

Git supports two remote transports for general use—the ssh transport and the HTTP transport. Of these, the ssh transport is much easier to set up, since most systems already have an ssh server package installed, configured, and ready to accept authenticated connections. This is generally not true for HTTP, and even if an HTTP server was available, you'd still have to configure it for Gitolite.

Therefore, we will explore adding and removing users for a server using the ssh transport. Some of the earlier chapters have already shown you the basics of how to add a user. It is now time to dig a little deeper into this and explore a few nuances and special cases.

Adding users

Strictly speaking, Gitolite doesn't know where users come from. If you recall the section on authentication and authorization from the previous chapter, you learned that Gitolite does not even do authentication—it leaves it up to the ssh server (or perhaps the HTTP server). However, Gitolite does help with ssh-based authentication, since that is the most common use of Gitolite, and the server and its configuration are fairly standard and predictable, in most cases.

A word of warning: do *not* add new users manually on the server. Gitolite users, repositories, and access rules are maintained by making changes to a special repository called `gitolite-admin` and pushing those changes to the server, as explained in *Chapter 2, Installing Gitolite*. Thus, almost everything you do will be within a clone of the `gitolite-admin` repository.

To add a user, say Alice, obtain her public key (typically $HOME/.ssh/id_rsa.pub on her workstation). Then copy it to the directory called keydir (in your clone of the gitolite-admin repository), with the username as the basename (for example, alice.pub for user alice). Finally, add the key using git add keydir/alice.pub, then commit and push.

Here are some additional points to note in order to do this correctly:

- All public key files must have names ending in .pub, and must be in openssh's default format.
- Usernames must start with an alpha-numeric character, and can then contain alpha-numerics, hyphens, underscores, periods, and the @ sign. Examples of valid usernames are sitaram, sitaram.chamarty, sitaramc@gmail.com, and so on.

Behind the scenes

Here's how Gitolite on the server processes users and keys. These actions are initiated from within a post-update hook for the gitolite-admin repository that Gitolite installs.

1. Gitolite reads the authorized keys file ($HOME/.ssh/authorized_keys), and makes a note of all the non-Gitolite keys (that is, keys that did not come from Gitolite).

2. It then reads all the public keys in the keydir directory of the gitolite-admin repository. This is recursive; you can have keys in subdirectories to any level.

3. As it reads each public key, it compares it to each of the public keys it has processed so far, including the non-Gitolite keys. If there is a match, it prints a warning to the effect that the ssh server will be ignoring the second and subsequent occurrences of the key in the authorized keys file.

4. It then adds ssh options to each public key line. The options added are no-port-forwarding, no-X11-forwarding, no-agent-forwarding, no-pty. These security options are generally recommended for any ssh server that is *not* meant to be serving interactive or shell users.

5. The command option is added, pointing to the installed gitolite-shell location, along with an additional argument: the Gitolite username. The username is usually the basename of the public key file (that is, removing any directory prefixes, and the .pub suffix); see the section on *Users with multiple key pairs* later when this may not be quite true.

If you recall from *Figure 1* in *Chapter 2, Installing Gitolite* (reproduced below for convenience), this ensures that when the user accesses the server and offers the corresponding public key for authentication, his connection, after the ssh daemon has successfully authenticated him, will be passed onto the `gitolite-shell` program, with his Gitolite username as a command-line argument.

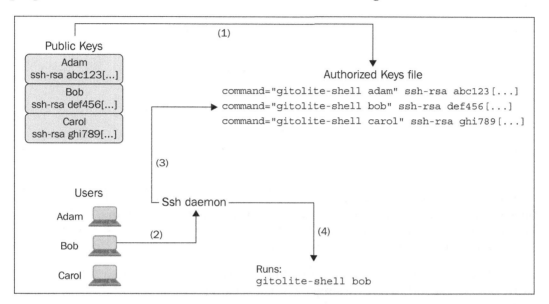

Users with multiple key pairs

Some users have multiple key pairs. For instance, they use a laptop as well as a desktop at work. Some may have another machine at home, or work directly on a server.

You might think it's best to use the same key pair on each machine—after all, they all belong to the same user—but this is not a good idea. The risk of a private key compromise increases with the number of machines that it is installed on, and that would not be a good thing at all.

As a result, Gitolite allows a user to have multiple public keys. There are in fact two ways to associate multiple public key files to the same Gitolite user.

The first way is to use subdirectories. Here's an example tree structure of the gitolite-admin repository showing a set of keys in the `keydir` subdirectory:

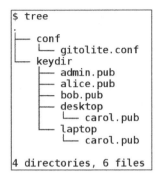

```
$ tree
.
├── conf
│   └── gitolite.conf
└── keydir
    ├── admin.pub
    ├── alice.pub
    ├── bob.pub
    ├── desktop
    │   └── carol.pub
    └── laptop
        └── carol.pub

4 directories, 6 files
```

As you can see, there are two files called `carol.pub`. Both of these will generate lines in the authorized keys file as described earlier, with the username set to `carol`. Whichever key she uses, Gitolite will see the authenticated Gitolite username as `carol`, and authorize her access accordingly.

The second way to allow multiple public keys is to use a location suffix. A location suffix is an @ sign followed by a single word consisting of alphanumerics, hyphens, or underscores. For example, if Alice had one key for her laptop and one for her desktop, she might send you the keys as `alice@laptop.pub` and `alice@desktop.pub`.

The location suffix must *not* contain a period; otherwise it looks like an e-mail address. As far as Gitolite is concerned, a public key file called `alice@laptop.pub` pertains to a user called alice, but a file called `alice@lap.top.pub` pertains to a user called `alice@lap.top`, which is a perfectly valid email address at least as far as syntax is concerned.

Giving some users a shell

Some of your users may have a legitimate need to log on to the server as the hosting user and use a shell command line. If this is required for just one or two users, the simplest way to deal with this is to have them use two different keys—one for Gitolite access and one for shell access. The second key would be installed manually in the authorized keys file on the server, and would not have the command and other options that Gitolite keys have.

 Non-Gitolite keys must be added right at the start of the authorized keys file, or at least before the marker line that says # gitolite start. Keys added in between Gitolite's start and end marker lines will be deleted the next time the gitolite-admin repository is pushed.

However, this requires careful handling of the second key on both the server side, as well as the client side. Some users may not be interested in learning how to handle multiple keys on their side, and how to present the correct key for each access.

There is another way to handle this problem, using a single key. Here's what you need to do in order to give any user shell access.

First, determine who is to get this access and make a list of those users. The username should be the bare username as used in the gitolite.conf file, for example, alice and bob. Do not use alice.pub, alice@laptop.pub, or any such variants.

Next, add all these names to a simple file called $HOME/.gitolite.shell-users on the server. Put just one name on each line, without any extra spaces before or after.

Then, edit the file $HOME/.gitolite.rc on the server, and uncomment the following lines:

```
# SHELL_USERS_LIST           =>   "$ENV{HOME}/.gitolite.shell-users",
```

and

```
# 'Shell',
```

Finally, run the following command:

```
gitolite trigger POST_COMPILE
```

Managing keys outside Gitolite

You do not have to let Gitolite manage the keys if you have a different method of managing them that you prefer. For example, you may be using an LDAP-backed ssh daemon, which manages users' keys centrally for several enterprise applications and systems, and therefore you wish to take advantage of that for Gitolite user management.

Gitolite will work fine with any method as long as you ensure that these points are covered:

- The SSH_ORIGINAL_COMMAND environment variable should contain the original Git command that the client sent out. Typically, this will be something like git-upload-pack 'repo.git' (including the single quotes) or, for pushes, git-receive-pack 'repo.git'.

  This variable is automatically set by the ssh daemon when the ssh configuration specifies a forced command of some kind (please see the ssh documentation for details on how to force commands).

- The command that is thus forced to run should be the full path to the gitolite-shell program, wherever you may have installed it. For example, it could be /home/git/gitolite/src/gitolite-shell.

- This program should get exactly one argument: the Gitolite username of the ssh-authenticated user.

Getting user group information from LDAP

Gitolite makes it possible to make some limited use of user data that may already be available in the enterprise.

The most common use case for this is that the enterprise already has an LDAP database that contains all the users and their roles in the organization. What the administrator would like to do is to use this information to reduce the burden of giving users rights to Gitolite repositories. It would be great if the administrator could merely specify rights in terms of group-names and Gitolite were to somehow figure out which groups a user is a member of.

Gitolite can facilitate the querying of the LDAP database and somehow acquire the information it needs. The solution involves writing a helper program, which does the following:

- Accept one Gitolite user ID as the first (and only) argument
- If necessary, convert this user ID in some unspecified manner to make it suitable for the LDAP query. For example, you may have to add specific components to the name for the query to work.
- Use this user ID as a query parameter and query the LDAP database to get user details. The program that does this will need to have credentials and permission to query the LDAP database.
- Once the query returns, extract the user's role/group information from the result.
- If required, again convert this group information to the names that you have used in Gitolite's access rules.
- Print the list of groups that result, all on one line and separated by spaces.

Once this program is done, save it as $HOME/bin/ldap-query-groups and test it. It's only taking one command-line argument and printing results to the terminal so there is no real harm in doing so, as far as Gitolite is concerned.

After testing it, edit Gitolite's rc file ($HOME/.gitolite.rc) and add the following line (including the trailing comma) somewhere within the definition of the %RC variable, preferably close to the top:

```
GROUPLIST_PGM            =>   "$ENV{HOME}/bin/ldap-query-groups",
```

Removing users

Removing Gitolite users is pretty simple. Just remove all the keys pertaining to the user (in case they have more than one, as discussed in an earlier section) from a clone of the gitolite-admin repository. This should be done using the git rm command, not a plain rm command.

After that, commit the change and push it.

You can confirm the removal in a couple of different ways. First, the keys you just removed should no longer be available in $HOME/.gitolite/keydir on the server. Second, the user should not be found if you search for the name in the authorized keys file ($HOME/.ssh/authorized_keys).

Summary

In this chapter, we saw how to add and remove users, as well as how to handle several other unusual requirements that may come up once in a while. In the next chapter, we will talk about adding and removing repositories.

5
Managing Repositories

One of the advantages of using Gitolite is that you do not need to create new repositories manually, set their permissions, and so on. Gitolite does all this for you, based on the contents of a specific file (`conf/gitolite.conf`) in the gitolite-admin repository. In this chapter, we will show how you can add new repositories to Gitolite, as well as how to bring in existing repositories in to Gitolite's ambit.

Adding repositories

To add a new repository, you will need to do the following in your clone of the gitolite-admin repository.

First, edit the `conf/gitolite.conf` file. This file should have some content already, for example:

```
repo    gitolite-admin
    RW+    =    adam
repo    testing
    RW+    =    @all
```

This basically says that only the user called `adam` has the permission to make changes to the `gitolite-admin` repository, and all users have the permission to make changes to the testing repository.

To add a new repository, you will need to add a repo line, as well as at least one access control rule. For example:

```
repo    my-repo-1
    RW+    =    adam
```

This will create a repository called `my-repo-1`, making `adam` the only user who can read or write it.

If you do not add an access rule, the repository is not created. For example, if you had the following:

```
repo    my-repo-1
repo    my-repo-2
    RW+    =    adam
```

then the my-repo-1 repository is neither created, not even recognized by Gitolite in any way.

However, you can specify more than one repository name in the repo line, so the following command is perfectly fine:

```
repo    my-repo-1 my-repo-2
    RW+    =    adam
```

Adding existing repositories

Adding a repository, as described in the previous section, will create an empty, bare, repository on the server. You can then populate that repository by pushing whatever content you like. This is certainly one way to bring existing content under Gitolite's control, as long as those repositories did not have their own Git hooks in place earlier.

However, most sites will have several existing repositories that need to be brought under Gitolite's control, and the technique of creating an empty repository and pushing content from a workstation can be really slow, especially if the content is already available on the server. This section will tell you how to do this quickly and easily.

 It is always advisable to have backups so that you can recover if something unexpected happens while following the procedure described.

First, make sure the existing repositories you are looking at are bare repositories. A bare Git repository is a repository that does not have a working tree. You cannot reliably push to a repository that has a working tree attached, so server repositories must always be bare. A bare repository is usually created by passing the --bare option to the git init or git clone commands. A later section in this chapter describes how to convert non-bare repositories to bare repositories.

Next, move or copy the bare repositories to $HOME/repositories, which is where Gitolite expects to find all the repositories it is managing. When doing this, make sure the name of the repository ends in .git.

 In common Git usage, it is merely a convention to name bare repositories with names ending in .git, while non-bare repositories do not have an extension. With Gitolite however, the trailing .git is necessary; it is no longer just a convention.

Once you have all the repositories in place, run the gitolite setup command.

Finally, in a clone of the gitolite-admin repository, add these repositories to the conf/gitolite.conf file as described earlier, save the changes, add, commit, and push.

Common problems and troubleshooting

You may need to modify the procedure described earlier under some circumstances. This section will describe some of the problems that you may find and how to work around them.

Ownership and permissions

Gitolite expects that all the files and directories inside $HOME/repositories are owned by the Gitolite hosting user, and that this user is allowed to write to all of them. If this condition is not met, both Git and Gitolite will be affected.

The most common reason for such a condition to be violated is that the administrator has copied some files (such as a bunch of existing repositories perhaps) as root. When files are copied as root, they are not usually given the owner and group ID of the directory in which they are being placed, but that of the original owner or the user executing the copy.

You can see this by running ls -alR on the repository in question; if the owner and group of all the files and directories are not git (the hosting user), then you will need to modify the ownership of that repository.

To fix this, run the following command: (As in earlier chapters, we assume the Gitolite hosting user is git; if not, please substitute accordingly.)

```
# as root
cd ~git
chown -R git:git repositories
chmod -R u+rwX repositories
```

If there are no ownership problems, but for some reason you do have permission issues, you can omit the chown command and do the rest as git (that is, you do not need to log in as root).

Converting a non-bare repository to a bare repository

A bare repository is a repository without the working tree attached to it. Instead, the files and directories that, in a non-bare repository, are contained within the special .git directory are directly placed in the repository at the top level.

One way to convert a non-bare repository to a bare repository is to clone it using the --bare option. The following command is the most generic way of doing this:

```
git clone –bare /somewhere/repo ~/repositories/repo.git
```

However, this makes a full copy of the source to the target, which might be a problem if the repository is very large. But if the source repository is on the same filesystem as the target, there is a very useful optimization that Git provides, which you can take advantage of. This is affected by adding a -l option to the clone command:

```
git clone –bare -l ~/somewhere/repo ~/repositories/repo.git
```

The -l option tells Git to use hardlinks instead of copying the files over to the new repository, and is almost instantaneous, regardless of how big the repository actually is. Since it uses hardlinks (and not symlinks), you are free to delete the source repository after the clone is done; it will not harm the newly created target repository.

Either way, at this point you will need to copy any hooks that already exist in your repository from the hooks directory of the source to that of the destination. This is because the clone method does not carry the hooks over.

Git experts will realize that another way to convert a non-bare repo, say my-repo, is to promote the .git directory up one level, renaming it my-repo.git. That is, by running the command mv my-repo/.git my-repo.git. At this point, the old my-repo directory can be deleted. As always, make sure you have backups before deleting anything.

Gitolite and the update hook

Gitolite's access control mechanism for a push operation involves hooking into Git's `update` hook mechanism (see the man page for `githooks` to get details on the various hooks that Git provides).

Therefore, if your existing repository already had an update hook, running the `gitolite setup` described previously will wipe out this existing hook and install Gitolite's own update hook in its place.

Gitolite *does* provide a mechanism that allows your old `update` hook to also run, but it needs to be run by Gitolite. There is a supported mechanism for this called VREF, which will be described briefly in *Chapter 7, Advanced Access Control and Configuration*, and in detail in *Chapter 10,* Understanding *VREFs*.

Summary

This chapter showed you how to add your own repositories, and told you about some common problems that may occur when bringing in existing repositories in to Gitolite's control. The previous chapter has already covered adding users, so we are now ready to start looking at access control. Access control is the reason Gitolite exists, and the next chapter will (finally!) show you some basic access control syntax, rules, and other details.

6
Getting Started with Access Control

By now, you know how to add new users to the Gitolite system, as well as how to create new repositories or bring existing repositories into Gitolite control. It's time to tie those together now and look at *access control*, which is, for most sites, the main reason to install Gitolite.

Basic access control examples

The aspect of access control that first comes to mind, for any Git administrator, is the ability to prevent people from accessing repositories. We'll start with some simple examples before describing the syntax. Here's a very simple set of rules for a repository called foo:

```
repo foo
    R    =   alice
    RW   =   bob
    RW+  =   carol
```

These rules establish what operations Alice, Bob, Carol, and any other Gitolite users are allowed to execute against this repository. As you might guess from the simple R permission given to Alice (or, to put it another way, the lack of a W in her permission string), she is only allowed to read the repository, which means she can use the git clone, git fetch, and git ls-remote commands, but cannot use git push in any form.

Bob and Carol are both allowed to push changes to the repository. As before, you probably guessed this from the W character in each of their permission lines. What may not be immediately obvious is the significance of the + character in Carol's permission string. This extra character allows Carol to *force* a push, that is, push a new object to a ref even if the new object is not a descendant of the old object. This is called a non-fast forward push in Git parlance, and, even in normal Git use (that is, even without an access control system in place), requires explicit action on the user's part in order to succeed. If you're not familiar with this, please consult man `git-push` and other Git resources.

The + character was chosen because it is a reminder of the + you have to use in the `git push` command to selectively force-push some refs. (Please refer to the description of the `refspec` field in the man page for the `git push` command for more details). Although we will not encounter this use case in this chapter, for the sake of completeness, we should also mention that the + character also allows a user to *delete* a ref, even though the corresponding syntax in the `git push` command does not use a + sign.

For a lot of installations, this basic example serves all their needs—namely, to distinguish people who are only allowed to read but not to write, and among those that are allowed to write, prevent some from dangerously force-pushing (or worse, deleting) an important branch or tag.

Basic branch level access control

The next example will show another very common need: that of restricting some people (perhaps junior developers or interns) to being able to push only branches in a specific namespace. This is a fairly common situation, where the most important branches (such as master, or maybe next, or whatever your branch naming and workflow uses), can only be changed by trusted developers, who presumably have reviewed the code and found it to be acceptable. Code written by junior developers and/or interns is not deemed to be automatically acceptable, and it is often useful to *sandbox* them in some way.

Interestingly, this particular use case appears to be more about developer trust and maturity than about security per se. However, in terms of controlling or preventing such behavior, there is no difference between someone accidentally overwriting the master branch, and someone doing it with malicious intent.

Here's an example of an access control rule set that achieves such a restriction:

```
repo foo
    R           =  alice
    RW+         =  bob
    RW+  dev/   =  carol
```

This allows Carol to read the repository as well as to push to it, but it prevents her from pushing anything except branches whose names start with dev/. In contrast, Bob whose access rule does not specify anything after the permission field, can push any branch.

Lexical syntax of the conf file

Now that we've seen a couple of useful, and immediately usable, examples, it is time to look at the **lexical** syntax of the conf/gitolite.conf file (often called, in Gitolite, *the conf file*).

The conf file is a plain text file, whose overall syntax is governed by a few simple rules.

Gitolite usernames (in our example, alice, bob, and so on) must start with an alphanumeric character, and contain alphanumerics, periods, hyphens, underscores, or the @ sign. If an @ sign is present, it must be followed by a domain name (that is, something that has at least one period in it). This allows e-mail addresses to be used as usernames, which is arguably very useful when you have several John Smith in your organization!

Repository names must start with an alphanumeric character, and contain alphanumerics, periods, hyphens, underscores, or slashes. However, they must not start with a slash or end with a slash.

Comments are allowed; the syntax is the same as the shell, perl, and so on. Anything following a # sign is taken to be a comment and discarded.

Continuation lines (in the C-style) are not allowed by default. However, by editing the $HOME/.gitolite.rc file, which we will see in more detail in *Chapter 7, Advanced Access Control and Configuration*, you can enable this feature.

The syntax of access control rules

The access control list has a simple structure. Briefly, it is structured like this:

```
repo <one or more repos or repo-groups>
    <permission>    <zero or more refexes>  =  <one or more users or
user-groups>
```

A conf file has one or more `repo` lines. Each repo line contains the word `repo`, followed by one or more repository names or repository-group names (we'll discuss groups later in this chapter). These repository or group names must all be on the same line.

Each `repo` line is followed by one or more *access rules* that apply to this set of repositories or groups. An access rule consists of the following:

- A permission field (for example, R, RW, and so on)
- Zero or more *refexes* (refexes are detailed in the next section, but one example refex you have already seen is `dev/`)
- An = sign to serve as a separator
- And finally a list of users or user-group names

Branch level access control and refexes

This section will talk about a very important part of Gitolite—specifying who can make changes to which branch or tag. As a matter of historical interest, the lack of this feature, in what was at that time the most popular tool for Git server administration, was the sole motivation for Gitolite being created.

 This section assumes some familiarity with *regular expressions*.

To understand branch level access control and how to specify them in Gitolite, we should first have a quick refresher of related concepts in Git itself, to make things easier to understand.

Git uses the word `ref` to refer to both branches and tags. Branch names are usually of the form `refs/heads/something`, while tag names are of the form `refs/tags/something`. When a user pushes to a Gitolite managed repository, Gitolite helps you determine whether the *refs* being updated are allowed to be updated by this user or not.

Thus, to allow Bob to push the branch called master, you might write:

```
RW+  refs/heads/master  =  bob
```

When a user pushes to the repository, Git supplies Gitolite with the name of the ref being pushed. Gitolite then matches the ref with each of the refexes in the access rule lines. If there is a match, and the user is also listed on the right side of the = sign, then the push is allowed.

However, due to the fact that branches are far more frequently access controlled than tags, Gitolite assumes anything that does not start with refs/ to be prefixed with refs/heads/. Thus, you can just say:

```
RW+  master   =  bob
```

and that would be taken as refs/heads/master.

To be strictly accurate, the preceding data allows Bob to push any branch with a name that starts with master. To restrict the rule to just master, you should actually write the refex as master$. In practice, however, this is rarely required.

Controlling tags is just as easy. Let us say you want to allow a user to push any tag with a name starts with the letter v, followed by a digit, optionally followed by anything else. Here's the rule for it:

```
RW+  refs/tags/v[0-9]  =  bob
```

The regular expression pattern [0-9] represents the notion of any character between 0 and 9 inclusive.

Gitolite anchors this regex at the beginning only, not at the end. In regex terms, this means a ^ character is implicitly added at the start, but a $ character is not added at the end. This allows Bob to push tags like v1, v2.2, v3.4.5, and so on, but not new-v1 and next-v2.

Thus we come to the definition of a *refex*: a refex is a regex (that is, a regular expression) that is used to match the ref being pushed.

Using deny rules

So far, the rules we have seen allow you to specify which branches or tags a user is allowed to push. However, we often need to be able to specify, for example, that a user is allowed to push *all branches except master*.

To do that, we need to use what Gitolite calls *deny* rules. Here's how you might implement the above restriction for a user:

```
-          master   =  bob
RW+                 =  bob
```

Gitolite checks rules in sequence when attempting to determine whether a branch is allowed to be pushed or not. When Bob pushes a branch called `next` (that is, `refs/heads/next`) to this repository, the first rule does not match at all, since `refs/heads/master` is not a pattern that matches the string `refs/heads/next`. Gitolite then checks the next rule. Since this rule does not specify a refex, all refs will match, and since the permission field is `RW+`, the push is allowed.

However, when Bob pushes `refs/heads/master`, the ref matches the refex in the first rule, and since the rule is a deny rule, the push is denied.

Observant readers will notice that the sequence of the rules is very important here. Reversing the order of the two rules we looked at would remove the restriction we want to implement. The first rule encountered will be:

```
RW+        =  bob
```

This does not specify a refex and thus matches all refs. As a result, the operation is allowed to proceed. In other words, the deny rule is never even checked!

The permission field

We have now seen examples of the four most common permissions used in access rules, so it is a good idea to summarize them.

The `R` permission allows the user to read (clone, fetch) the repository, but not push. `RW` allows the user to push, but only if it is a fast-forward push or a new branch is being created. Non-fast forward pushes and deletions are not allowed. And `RW+` allows non-fast forward pushes and deletions too.

As long as your rule set contains only these three types of rules, it does not matter which order they appear in. However, as you saw in the previous section, the sequence of rules becomes important when you use the fourth kind of rule—a deny rule, denoted by a single minus sign.

> While these are the most commonly used permissions, they are not all there are. There are a few more permissions which will appear in the section *Types of Write Operations* in *Chapter 7, Advanced Access Control and Configuration.*

Defining user and repo groups

Gitolite allows you to define groups of users or repositories for convenience. The syntax is very simple, and does not distinguish between a user group and a repository group. For example, take a look at the deny rule example in the previous section:

```
-           master    = bob
RW+                   = bob
```

Let's say that, instead of just Bob, you had several more users who must be prevented from pushing the master branch, perhaps because they are all junior developers. One way is to add each of their usernames on both the rule lines, after Bob's username, like this:

```
-           master    = bob carol dave
RW+                   = bob carol dave
```

But this gets cumbersome, and will only get worse if there are more rules to be applied to the same group of people.

With groups, however, you can do this:

```
@junior-devs    = bob carol dave


-           master    = @junior-devs
RW+                   = @junior-devs
```

As you can see, this is far more convenient, and also less error-prone. Even more importantly, the group name can often serve as important documentation for the ruleset—a future administrator may not know who Bob, Carol, and Dave are, and may puzzle over why they were restricted, but the group name, if chosen well, makes things very clear.

You can use group names for repositories also, for example:

```
@foss-repos  = git linux apache gcc


repo @foss-repos
  R  = @all
```

While in this case it may not look as critical, because the group name is being used to replace only one occurrence of the repository names, it is still a lot cleaner. Also, as with the user group names, the repository group name serves as additional documentation of the nature of those repositories.

Working with large groups

Sometimes you need a group which contains several members — far more than can fit on one line comfortably to edit. To make this easier (and because Gitolite does not, by default, allow continuation lines), Gitolite treats every definition of a group as cumulative. This means that if the group was already defined earlier, the new members are added to it rather than replacing the existing member list. This allows you to say:

```
@foss-repos   =   git
@foss-repos   =   linux
@foss-repos   =   apache
```

This would have the same effect as the single line definition we saw earlier in this section.

The special @all group

Gitolite also has a special, built-in group called @all, which refers to all repositories, or all users, depending on where it is used. A common use for this is to allow certain privileged users access to all repositories, perhaps as follows:

```
repo @all
    R             =   @QA-leads
    RW+           =   @dev-leads
```

For another example, let us consider a situation where only Adam and Dave are allowed to push the master branch. Here's how you might do that:

```
repo foo
    RW+  master         =   adam dave
    -          master   =   @all
```

We have a *deny* rule here, so again, notice that the order of rules is important. If we had placed the *deny* rule first, then — because Adam and Dave are implicitly members of @all — they would also be denied rights to push the master branch.

The include statement

You can also split up your access rules and group definitions into multiple files, and *include* them into the main conf file (`conf/gitolite.conf` in your gitolite-admin repository). For example, you can keep all group information (that is, which users are members of which groups) in a separate file and include that. The syntax is very simple; here's an example:

```
include "groups.conf"
```

This will look for a file called `groups.conf` in the `conf` directory and include its contents at that point.

Advanced users may note that this command also accepts wildcards. For example, you might have several individual conf files in a subdirectory of `conf` called `foss`. If you don't want to name each of them separately, you can say:

```
include "foss/*.conf"
```

Rule accumulation and delegation

Gitolite allows you to split up access rules for repositories into multiple chunks which are not necessarily contiguous. It will then combine all these chunks (in the order they were read) and apply the combined set of rules to the repository in question.

There's a very good use for this behavior. Combining groups, that include statement, and rule accumulation, makes Gitolite administration easier than it already is. Here's an example, with some comments, to give you some idea of what can be done.

```
include "groups.conf"
# contains definitions of all groups used in the rest of the conf file.
All
# membership changes happen here

include "foss.conf"
# contains rules for open source repositories.  For example, "R = @all" is
# pretty much expected for such repositories.  There may be other rules
# specific to different FOSS repositories that may also be specified here

include "boss.conf"
# contains rules that define what kind of access management has to the
```

```
# development repositories.  For example, some of the managers may have
# read access to all repositories, so something like
#     repo @all
#       R  =  scott douglas
# is probably quite useful.

# repo-specific rules
# At this point you could have repository specific rules that do not fit
neatly
# into any of the previous include files.  For example:
repo git
  RW+  =  linus junio
```

As you can see, a repository can appear in any or all of the include files that the main conf file pulls in. If we required all the rules for each repository to be in one place, it would be impossible to organize your rules in this sort of manner.

Summary

We've now seen most of Gitolite's basic access control features, including various types of access rules, the syntax of the conf file, and some convenient features that make managing this easier. In the next chapter, we will discuss some advanced access control features, such as personal branches and **VREFs**.

7
Advanced Access Control and Configuration

The basic access control methods described in the previous chapter are sufficient for most sites, and there are many that do not go further than that. However, Gitolite has a lot more features waiting for people who need them. We'll go through some of these advanced features in this chapter. In each case, we'll attempt to describe a practical scenario that demonstrates a need and then explain how the feature fulfills that need.

Making changes to the rc file

Many of Gitolite's advanced features and configuration options are managed by editing the *rc file*. This is a file named `.gitolite.rc`, which is present in the home directory of the Gitolite hosting user.

The file is liberally commented and it is generally easy to see where things go.

The bulk of the file is within a top-level definition that looks as follows:

```
%RC = (
...several variables defined...
)
```

If you're familiar with Perl, you might realize that this is a Perl hash, but it is not necessary to know Perl in order to edit this file.

The file has several simple variables defined, for example:

```
UMASK                          =>   0077,
```

When the Gitolite documentation (or this book) tells you to edit a variable in the rc file, it's best to look for such a variable first—most of the important ones are already in the file but may be commented out, waiting to be un-commented and the value edited as needed.

One of the variables within the %RC block is a list variable called ENABLE, whose definition looks as follows:

```
ENABLE => [
...several features listed...
]
```

An example feature is as follows:

```
        'info',
```

This enables the info command.

Again, most features are already listed here, but may be commented out.

Giving users their own branches

When there are more than a few developers in a project, it is often necessary for them to share code that is still under development, for comments, discussion, preliminary testing, and so on. The obvious solution is for each developer to push to a branch on the Gitolite server and inform his colleagues of the branch name. A branch namespace dedicated to this can be created, giving all developers access to it, as follows:

```
repo foo
    RW+    sandbox/  =  @developers
```

This works fine, but it could lead to a situation where one developer accidentally overwrites or deletes another developer's branch if the branch naming within the *sandbox* namespace is not strictly controlled.

What is required, ideally, is something as follows:

```
    RW+    sandbox/alice/  =  alice
    RW+    sandbox/bob/    =  bob
```

and so on, for each user who should be given access to the repository.

Clearly, this is not at all scalable—you'd have to add one line for each user if you did this. In fact, it's a step backward because we've suddenly lost all the advantages of managing users in groups, since we are forced to use a separate rule for each developer.

This situation is what led to the development of what are called **personal branches** in Gitolite. This feature works on a simple idea, and is best described with the following example rule:

```
RW+    sandbox/USER/  =  @developers
```

The idea is that the word USER, surrounded by slashes, stands for the authenticated username from the connection information, as long as the user is listed on the right-hand side (or a group he/she belongs to is listed). Thus, if the user ID alice is a member of the @developers group, and Alice attempts to access the repository, this rule effectively becomes the following:

```
RW+    sandbox/alice/   =  alice
```

This allows Alice to write to her own sandbox branches; that is, branches whose names start with sandbox/alice/. Note that this does not allow a branch called sandbox/alice — the sandbox is meant to be a set of branches not just one branch.

Since Gitolite does not allow limiting read access by branch, every user who is a member of the @developers group has read access to the repository, which means they can read each other's development branches, but only write (push to) their own sandbox branches.

Types of write operations

So far, we have restricted ourselves to the RW and RW+ permissions while talking about permissions. The former gives users permission to create new branches and tags, and make **fast forward** pushes to the branches, while the latter allows users to also make non-fast forward pushes and rewrite tags, as well as delete branches and tags.

> This is by far the most common situation, and this syntax serves for the vast majority of access control needs. A push to an existing tag, even if the new commit is a descendent of the current commit the tag is pointing to, is still considered a non-fast forward push. This is because, unlike branches, tags are not *meant* to be moved; once written, they're supposed to be fixed and never change.

However, in some situations, you may need to explicitly specify the ability to *create* a branch, separating it from that of pushing a new commit to it. Similarly, you may want to explicitly specify permission to *delete* a branch or tag, separating it from that of pushing a non-fast forward commit; or, you may want to do both.

In order to achieve this, Gitolite has an extended syntax for the permissions field to let you specify explicit create and/or delete permissions. Using these extended permissions in any rule applicable to a repository has the effect of limiting the power of the normal RW and RW+ permissions, in terms of creating or deleting refs.

This extended syntax consists of the following *new permissions*: RWC, RW+C, RWD, RW+D, RWCD, and RW+CD. When a rule specifying a permission containing a C is added to a repository, the RW and RW+ rules for that repository no longer permit *creating* a branch or a tag. Similarly, when any rule specifies a permission containing a D, the RW+ rules for that repository no longer allow *deleting* a ref. For ease of discussion, we can call these the *explicit create* and *explicit delete* modes, respectively.

It is useful to summarize these rules in a tabular form, for ready reference in case you ever need to use these special permission modes. The following table shows you the minimum required permission "characters" to allow a given operation, in each of the three modes (strictly speaking, there is a fourth mode, where both explicit create and explicit delete are used, but that is just a combination of the two):

	Default mode	Explicit create mode	Explicit delete mode
Create new branch	RW	RW and C	RW
Create new tag	RW	RW and C	RW
Fast forward push existing branch	RW	RW	RW
Non-fast forward push a branch	RW+	RW+	RW+
Overwrite an existing tag	RW+	RW+	RW+
Delete branch	RW+	RW+	RW and D
Delete tag	RW+	RW+	RW and D

Allowing Gitweb and Git-daemon access

Gitweb (and, to a lesser extent, **git-daemon**) are popular tools that provide alternative, read-only access to Git repositories. Git-daemon provides completely unauthenticated access to Git repositories, suitable for open source or similar projects. Gitweb displays repositories, their branches, commit history, and many more details on a web browser. Gitweb itself does not do any authentication, but relies on the web server to authenticate users.

Gitweb and git-daemon have ways to determine which repositories are allowed to be made available to clients. For gitweb, the list of permitted repositories is placed in a specific format (at its simplest, one repository name per line) in a specific file at a configurable location (see the documentation for gitweb for details). On the other hand, git-daemon looks inside each individual repository for a file called `git-daemon-export-ok`, to determine if the repository should be made accessible to clients. Of course, both tools have other one-time configuration that needs to be handled and set up before they can be used. Gitweb, in particular, may not even run as the Gitolite hosting user, and the one-time setup will probably involve allowing it to read files owned by the Gitolite hosting user.

Although Gitolite cannot help in the one-time configuration of these tools, it can certainly help in managing the access list. It does this by designating two special Gitolite usernames: `gitweb` and `daemon`. These users do not have public keys, so they're not actual users in the same sense as Adam, Alice, or Bob in our examples. However, they determine which repositories are accessible by gitweb and git-daemon.

The idea is very simple. If you want a repository to be readable by gitweb, you give the `gitweb` user *read* access. Similarly, if you want the repository to be accessible via git-daemon, you give the `daemon` user *read* access. Here's an example that does both:

```
repo foo

    R  =  gitweb  daemon
```

Of course, instead of specifying each repository, you can use any repository group name that you may have defined, or even the special group name `@all`.

When the gitolite-admin repository is pushed, Gitolite checks each repository to see if these special users have been given read access. For each such repository, Gitolite adds the name to the projects list file mentioned previously if the `gitweb` user can read it, and creates a file called `git-daemon-export-ok` if the `daemon` user can. Also, if you previously allowed access and then decided to remove it, Gitolite will delete the entry from the projects list file, and/or remove the `git-daemon-export-ok` file, as applicable.

Locating the projects list file

We mentioned earlier that Gitweb consults a file containing a list of permitted repositories, and that Gitolite creates this file. Of course, Gitweb and Gitolite must agree on where this file is. Gitolite places it, by default, in `$HOME/projects.list`, but this can be changed to any other location if needed; simply add a line like the following to the `$HOME/.gitolite.rc` file, substituting whatever path you want of course.

```
GITWEB_PROJECTS_LIST => "/path/to/projects.list",
```

The syntax of the preceding statement includes the trailing comma. This line must be placed in the section marked rc variables used by various features.

Unix permissions and the umask

Gitweb is invoked by your web server (such as Apache), which is almost certainly running under a different user ID than your Gitolite hosting user. Depending on your OS and your web server, this could be a user called apache, www-data, or something else.

This means you need to make sure that this user can read the files it needs (mainly the projects list file, and everything under $HOME/repositories). There are usually two ways of doing this. The simplest way is to do the following:

1. Identify the primary group that your Gitolite hosting user belongs to (usually the same as the username). You can find this by running the id command after logging in to the server as the Gitolite hosting user. On most systems, it is the same as the user ID, so for our discussion let's say it is git.

2. Identify the Unix user ID under which your web server is running. For our discussion, let's say it is apache.

3. Add the apache user to the git group using the usermod command. (You need to run this as root on your server.) The exact syntax may vary depending on your OS and OS version. As an example, the command on a Red Hat system is usermod -G git apache.

4. Change the UMASK value in $HOME/.gitolite.rc from the default 0077 to 0027.

5. Fix up existing files manually. This is a one-time operation, required because umask only affects permissions on newly created files, not existing ones. Log in as the Gitolite hosting user and run the command chmod -R g+rX $HOME/projects.list $HOME/repositories.

The second method to deal with this involves running gitweb as the Gitolite hosting user. Most web servers provide mechanisms to run specific programs under some other user ID than the user ID under which the web server is running, such as the suexec feature in the Apache web server. Configuring these features is out of scope for this book; please check the documentation of your web server for more information.

Specifying Git config values and Gitolite options

If you're familiar with Git, you probably know the `git config` command, which allows you to set repository options. Example of config variables that may be useful for server-side (bare) repositories are `core.logAllRefUpdates`, `receive.fsckObjects`, and various performance-related config variables. (Please see the man page for `git-config` for details)

Gitolite aims to allow almost all administration remotely, so it would be unreasonable to expect the admin to log on to the server and run the `git config` command. Therefore, Gitolite allows the admin to specify config settings within the conf file, as follows:

```
repo foo
    RW+                                 =   adam
    config      receive.fsckObjects     =   true
```

> However, before you can use this feature, you need to enable the config keys you wish to use in the *rc* file (`$HOME/.gitolite.rc`). Look in this file for a line that contains the word `GIT_CONFIG_KEYS` and edit the value, which is empty by default, to contain a space separated list of the config keys you are planning to use.

In general, the syntax is `config sectionname.keyname = value`. On the server, this is executed as `git config sectionname.keyname value`. Gitolite does *not* support any of the other forms of the `git config` command, especially keys with multiple values.

Deleting a git-config key

Unfortunately, once a git `config` key has been created by Gitolite, simply removing the line from the conf file will not, on the next push, delete the key from the repository config file. This is because you *are* permitted to add keys directly on the server if you choose to (or your repository may have inherited some useful settings when you migrated it into Gitolite's control). Gitolite has no simple way of distinguishing `config` keys you created manually from those that were deleted in the conf file; that is, it can be done but it's complicated and potentially error-prone.

Therefore, Gitolite requires the following syntax in order to explicitly delete a `config` key from the repository config file on the server:

```
config sectionname.keyname = ""
```

This is the only way to delete a `config` key using Gitolite.

Substituting the repository name

Sometimes you need the same config setting for multiple repositories, but you only need to vary the repository name itself. The obvious way seems to be to do the following:

```
repo foo
    config hooks.mailinglist = foo-commits@example.tld
    config hooks.emailprefix = "[foo] "
repo bar
    config hooks.mailinglist = bar-commits@example.tld
    config hooks.emailprefix = "[bar] "
```

But, of course, this does not scale at all!

Gitolite allows you to do the following instead:

```
repo foo bar
    config hooks.mailinglist = %GL_REPO-commits@example.tld
    config hooks.emailprefix = "[%GL_REPO] "
```

Gitolite expands the token `%GL_REPO` into each repository's name when actually applying the config lines.

> Don't forget that in the `repo` line, you can have one or more repository groups, or a combination of repositories and groups. You can also use `@all` if you wish.

Overriding config values

Sometimes, you want to add a config value to all the repositories, except one or two. For example, consider the `hooks.mailinglist config` variable shown earlier, and imagine that, while the setting is correct for most repositories, one specific repository needs a completely different mailing list.

Gitolite allows you to do this as follows. First the general setting applicable to all repositories is added. Then, specific settings for specific repositories are added. Gitolite will ensure that for any repository, the last seen config setting will be the one used (and therefore, the order of these statements matters):

```
repo @all
    config hooks.mailinglist = %GL_REPO-commits@example.tld
    config hooks.emailprefix = "[%GL_REPO] "
repo foo
    config hooks.mailinglist = foo-list@users.example.tld
```

You can even use an empty value for the last line, if you wish that the special repository mentioned does not even have the corresponding entry in its config file.

Gitolite options

Similar to Git's config keys and values, Gitolite also has its own set of internal options, which are used to modify its default behavior in some way or provide additional information that some feature may need. For example, if you use Gitolite's mirroring feature (discussed in *Chapter 11, Mirroring*), you will need to specify, for each repository, which server is the master server and which are the slaves. These server names are specified using Gitolite options, as follows:

```
repo foo
    option mirror.master    =    mars
    option mirror.slaves    =    phobos
```

When the mirroring code runs, it interrogates Gitolite for the value of these options in order to do its job.

Gitolite options behave just like the `config` entries, shown earlier, do in terms of later entries overriding earlier values.

Applying deny rules to read access

In the previous chapter, when we looked at the `deny` rules, we showed them only in the context of a write operation, controlling whether a certain branch or tag can be pushed or not.

By default, the deny rules are not examined when checking read access. So something like the following:

```
@junior-devs = alice bob carol

repo foo

    -               =   bob

    RW+             =   @junior-devs
```

will not prevent Bob from at least reading the repository (that is, using `git clone` or `git fetch`), even though the deny rule appears first.

However, it is possible to make Gitolite act on deny rules in this case also. This is achieved by specifying a Gitolite option called `deny-rules`, as follows:

```
repo foo

    -                       =   bob

    RW+                     =   @junior-devs

    option deny-rules       =   1
```

Now Bob will not even be able to clone the repository.

> It is also important to understand that, for read access, specifying an actual branch in the deny rule, shown as follows:
>
> ```
>     -           master  =   bob
>     RW+                 =   @junior-devs
> ```
>
> is the same as not having a branch in the rule. This is because Git (and therefore Gitolite) does not distinguish between branches for read access control, so any specified refex is ignored.

The `deny-rules` option will prevent write access the same way it prevents read access. It does not make sense to allow a user to write what they cannot read!

Understanding VREFs

The previous chapter introduced us to the concept of a *refex*, which is a regular expression that is used to match the ref being pushed. This allows us to make decisions on allowing or rejecting the push based on the name of the ref (branch or tag) being pushed.

However, we might have other criteria for deciding whether to allow or deny the push. The most common example is whether specific files have been changed, and if they have, to disallow the push.

A *VREF* is a special kind of refex; the "V" stands for "Virtual". This is a refex that will not match the ref that Git knows about (which is a branch name or a tag name). Rather, it will attempt to match against some other characteristic of the commit or series of commits being pushed.

Here's an example. Let's say you are running a project where the build system, and in particular the `Makefile`, is a rather critical component and has been finely tuned to play nicely with all the environments for which your product is built and sold. As a result, you really don't want anyone but the most experienced people messing with that file (and perhaps others related to it). You would, therefore, like to prevent your junior developers from being able to push changes to it. Here's how you would do that:

```
repo foo
    RW+                      =   @developers
    -   VREF/NAME/Makefile   =   @junior-developers
```

That is basically all you have to do. First, the ruleset is checked for the ref that is being pushed (in this example, we simplified all that by allowing all developers—which includes junior developers—to push any branch). Once this succeeds, the *VREFs* specified are checked in the order they appear in the list of rules.

A VREF rule has a simple structure, consisting of the word `VREF`, followed by the name of the VREF (in this case, `NAME`, which is a VREF that checks the names of changed files and directories), followed by an argument of some kind. The list of changed file names is matched against that argument, and if a match is found, it is just as if you were trying to push a branch and the refex matched, which is to say the permission in the rule line drives what happens next. In this example, that results in the push being denied.

This gives you a simple preview of the VREF feature. *Chapter 10, Understanding VREFs,* will go into much more detail about this powerful feature of Gitolite.

Summary

In this chapter, we looked at some of Gitolite's advanced features, such as personal branches, Git config variables, Gitolite options, and so on. The next chapter will focus on another very powerful and popular feature of Gitolite, allowing your users to create their own repositories without having to add anything new to the conf file.

8
Allowing Users to Create Repos

Until now, everything we have seen indicates that the administrator is the only person who can create new repositories. He can share the load of doing this, simply by giving some trusted users the right to read and write the gitolite-admin repository, but that's as far as it goes.

In some environments, your users may need more flexibility. You could have several users who need not be administrators, in the sense that they neither want nor need to manage *all* repositories, but they do wish to be able to create their own repositories and control access to those repositories. In fact, we would like the administrator's role in this to be a one-time setup, after which no more changes to Gitolite's *conf* file would be required.

If there are several users who need to do this, it seems like a good idea to think about how we could allow this and still maintain the required security over the repositories that were created by the administrator in the usual way.

In this chapter, we'll work out a solution to the problem described in the introduction. We'll begin by talking about some features that help us with parts of the solution, and then add the missing pieces one by one to build up a solution.

Putting repositories in Sub-directories

The first part of the solution is that, as was hinted at in the first chapter, Gitolite allows you to group repositories in subdirectories, just like you can do with files in a filesystem. For example, you could put all the open source projects you're managing under a subdirectory called `foss`, like the following:

```
repo foss/apache
     ...access rules for the apache repo...
repo foss/linux
     ...access rules for the linux repo...
...etc...
```

We can make use of this in solving our current problem. Let's say we had users Alice and Bob, and we wanted to let them create and manage repositories. We could come up with a way by which Alice's repositories would be in a subdirectory called, say, `dev/alice`, and Bob's repositories would, similarly, be within `dev/bob`.

Repository wildcards

A repository wildcard is a regular expression that describes a whole range of possible repository names. For example, the line `repo dev/alice/[a-z].*` represents all repositories whose names start with `dev/alice/`, followed by an alphabetic character, followed optionally by anything else. The repository `dev/alice/foo` would qualify, but `dev/alice/123` would not, nor would just `dev/alice`.

> Due to the need to properly represent repositories such as `gtk+` and `c++`, if the + character is the only regular expression metacharacter in the repo name, it will be taken to be a normal repository, not a repository wildcard. To specify `foo.+`, you should instead say `foo..*`. You can also say `[f]oo.+` — the presence of the bracket tells Gitolite it is a regular expression.

Gitolite allows `repo` lines to use wildcards instead of individual repository names. This gives us the next step to our solution; we can now write:

```
repo dev/alice/[a-z].*
    RW+       =   alice
    RW        =   bob
    R         =   @all
repo dev/bob/[a-z].*
    RW+       =   bob
    RW        =   alice
    R         =   @all
```

This says that Bob can push (but not rewind or delete) branches to all of Alice's repositories, and vice versa, and that other authenticated users of the system can clone both those sets of repositories.

Sadly, though, a wildcard repository specification by itself does not actually *create* any repositories, since the pattern itself can match billions of possible repository names!

Creating a wildcard repository

Now it's time to introduce the first part of the additional syntax that Gitolite provides to help in solving the problem we started this chapter with. As we noted, the wildcard specification lines don't actually create the repositories that Alice or Bob need.

To enable that, we add a new line to the access rules specification:

```
repo dev/alice/[a-z].*
    C    =    alice
    ...other rules stay the same...
repo dev/bob/[a-z].*
    C    =    bob
    ...other rules stay the same...
```

> This is different than the *create branch* permission we saw in the *Types of write operations* section in *Chapter 7, Advanced Access Control and Configuration*. The one described here is the single letter C by itself, while the other can only exist as a modifier to RW or RW+.

This access rule says that, merely by cloning or pushing a repository with a matching name, Alice *can cause repositories to be created on the server*! In other words, Alice can run the following command:

```
$ git clone  git@host:dev/alice/my-new-repo
Cloning into 'my-new-repo'...

Initialized empty Git repository in /home/git/repositories/dev/alice/my-
new-repo.git/

warning: You appear to have cloned an empty repository.
```

It would be as if the administrator had added a new set of rules as follows:

```
repo dev/alice/my-new-repo
    RW+       =   alice
    RW        =   bob
    R         =   @all
```

except that the administrator doesn't have to!

Don't miss the `Initialized empty...` line in the preceding output; that came from the server, telling you a brand new repository was created as a result of this clone! In addition, if Alice ran the `info` command, she might see something as follows:

```
$ ssh git@host info

hello alice, this is git@host running gitolite3 v3.5.3.1-7-g31d11b9 on
git 1.8.3.1


    C   dev/CREATOR/..*
  R W   dev/u1/my-new-repo
  R W   testing
```

which shows you the repository that was just created.

> A downside is that a simple typo can cause useless repositories to be created. If you wish to prevent this, edit `$HOME/.gitolite.rc` and uncomment the `create` command as well as the `no-auto-create` option. Then your users can run the more explicit `create` command, for example: `ssh git@host create dev/alice/my-new-repo`.

Giving access to other users

We have so far simply hardcoded the permissions—Alice and Bob have some access to each other's repositories, and everyone else can read both sets of repositories. This is clearly not flexible enough, Alice may want some repositories to be writable by David, and some should not be readable by `@all`, and so on.

On the face of it, this is a difficult problem because it seems to imply that Alice might want to actually make changes or additions to the rules themselves, and thus, directly or indirectly, touch Gitolite's *conf* file.

The way Gitolite solves these problems is to allow the administrator to define roles, and then allow the user to specify which users she wants in each role. The following is an example using role names that are defined by default in Gitolite:

```
repo dev/alice/[a-z].*
    C       =  alice
    RW+     =  alice
    RW      =  WRITERS
    R       =  READERS
```

READERS and WRITERS are role names that are predefined in Gitolite. Note that the role names themselves don't have any special meaning in terms of what access rights a role has—that is entirely up to the administrator.

At the moment, however, this is not complete. The rules do not actually say that Bob is a writer (and thus has RW permission on Alice's repositories) or that everyone else (@all) can read it.

This is where the perms command comes in. Here's how Alice would use it to add Bob to the WRITERS role:

```
ssh  git@host perms dev/alice/my-new-repo + WRITERS bob
```

Similarly, to add @all to the READERS role, she would run the following command:

```
ssh  git@host perms dev/alice/my-new-repo + READERS @all
```

If she wishes to check what the current role assignments for her repository are, she can run.

```
ssh  git@host perms -l dev/alice/my-new-repo
```

which will dutifully print:

```
READERS @all
WRITERS bob
```

One advantage you should see right away is that now the role assignment is *per repository*. That is, Alice can have completely different role assignments for other repositories she owns. In fact, if she does not run the perms command on a repository, no one else will have any access—it becomes her private repository. Or she can add multiple people to each role too if she wishes. The perms command can only be used to add one user to one role in one go. So Alice may have to run this multiple times. If she added someone whom she now wishes to remove, that is also possible. As normal for all Gitolite commands, perms responds to a single argument of -h to provide a usage message.

Generalizing the ruleset

We'll now look at the ruleset as it stands for each user, and then discuss how to generalize it to any number of users. At this point, if you recall from the previous section, the rules look as follows:

```
repo dev/alice/[a-z].*
     C        =  alice
     RW+      =  alice
     RW       =  WRITERS
     R        =  READERS
```

You might notice that other than the word alice in the first three lines being replaced by Bob, this is precisely what you need for Bob's repositories as well. It certainly does not make sense to have to repeat this for every user who might need this feature!

The final part of the solution to allowing users to create, and (to some extent) manage, their own repositories is the CREATOR keyword. Here's the canonical example again:

```
repo dev/CREATOR/[a-z].*
     C        =  alice bob carol dave
     RW+      =  CREATOR
     RW       =  WRITERS
     R        =  READERS
```

Notice the changes we made. First, the C permission line now lists all the users who are allowed to create their own repositories and manage it as we have described earlier. Only these four users can do this, in this ruleset. Alternatively, you can replace the four usernames with some group name that you may have defined, or even use @all to allow all authenticated users to use the facility of creating private repositories they can selectively open up to others.

Next, the repository name pattern contains CREATOR instead of alice, as does the RW+ line. For repositories that do not yet exist, these are effectively treated as the name of the user who's trying to create the repository. For existing repositories, this is treated as the name of the user who created it, which is recorded and kept track of.

When a repository does not exist, the only permission that Gitolite cares about is the C permission that allows creating a repository. Whoever is on the right side of such a rule is allowed to create repositories matching the pattern. One error to watch out for is to put in C = CREATOR, instead of a list of actual users or user groups. Because, as described above, this is treated as the name of user attempting to create the repository, this allows any authenticated user to create such a repository. If that is what you want, it's better to be clear and actually use @all instead of CREATOR; the latter is just a side-effect and not supported behavior.

Explaining wild repos to your users

Your users, of course, do not need all of this explanation! In fact, one of the goals of this feature is that Gitolite users (as opposed to Gitolite *administrators*) should *not* be burdened with learning the nuances of RW, RW+, *deny* rules, and so on.

The example setup we have been using till now is the canonical example: it contains an owner (who is the only user allowed to rewind or delete branches), a set of writers (who can push/create but not rewind/delete), and a set of readers who cannot push at all.

The only thing left to do is to explain to the user what repositories she is allowed to create (most users do not know regular expressions very well, so it's best to keep your patterns simple enough to be explained in English), and that she can add or remove people from each of those *lists of users*.

The list names (in our example, READERS and WRITERS) should be supplied, and explained as representing what the users in each list can do.

Finally, show them three examples of the perms command used to maintain these user lists:

- ssh git@host perms dev/alice/repo + WRITERS dave to add a user
- ssh git@host perms dev/alice/repo - WRITERS dave to remove a user (notice the minus sign instead of the plus sign)
- ssh git@host perms -l dev/alice/repo to list current user lists

Managing with just wild repos

If you think about the example we've been working on throughout this chapter, it does not allow the user to trust anyone *else* with RW+ permissions; if any rewinding or deleting of branches is required it has to be the owner herself that does it.

We can rectify this by changing the RW+ permission line to:

```
RW+     =    CREATOR TRUSTED
```

Thus, defining a new role (or list of users, if you will) called TRUSTED. Of course, for this to work, you—as the administrator—must log on to the server and edit $HOME/.gitolite.rc to add this new role to the list of roles defined in that file under the ROLES hash. Then you can tell your user that there is a third list of users, called TRUSTED, which she can use to specify users she would like to allow to rewind or delete branches or tags.

Now that we have started going this route, we can go a little further and then a little more, until we end up with something that is essentially a one-time setup of Gitolite, requiring little to no further maintenance, from the administrator, once it has been set up. This can be very useful in sites where most of the users are somewhat autonomous.

Here's a comprehensive example of such a ruleset. To make things easier to copy and use, we've added the description of the rulesets as comments so you can copy them too:

```
# completely private repo; no sharing even possible
repo private/CREATOR/..*
    C         =    @all
    RW+       =    CREATOR


# public template; anyone can read but writes only by owner
repo public/CREATOR/..*
    C         =    @all
    RW+       =    CREATOR
    R         =    @all


# a controlled repo with 3 roles allowing RW+, RW, and R
repo controlled/CREATOR/..*
    C         =    @all
    RW+       =    CREATOR
    RW+       =    TRUSTED
```

```
    RW          =   WRITERS
    R           =   READERS


# a "corporate" type template with managers, testers, etc.
# Junior devs cant write 'master', can't rewind.  Testers
# (and *only* testers) can push versioned tags.  Managers
# can read any repo.
repo corporate/CREATOR/..*
    C               =   @all
    RW+             =   CREATOR
    RW refs/tags/v[0-9]  =  TESTERS
    -  refs/tags/v[0-9]  =  @all
    RW+             =   SENIOR_DEVS
    -  master       =   JUNIOR_DEVS
    RW              =   JUNIOR_DEVS
    R               =   MANAGERS
```

Deleting wild repositories

With the example in the previous section, the administrator's job is much lightened (albeit at the expense of *some* loss of control). However, there still remains one feature that your users will eventually want: deleting repositories that have served their purpose.

In order to allow users to delete repositories that they have created (it need not be said that a user cannot delete anything else!), the administrator needs to enable the D command by uncommenting the corresponding line in the list of commands in $HOME/.gitolite.rc. Then the user can run the D command to delete repositories.

Repositories are locked against accidental deletion by default, so every delete is actually two steps — the unlock sub-command, then the rm sub-command:

```
ssh  git@host D unlock dev/alice/my-new-repo
ssh  git@host D rm dev/alice/my-new-repo
```

Summary

This may be one of the most important chapters in this book, since it talks about a very popular feature of Gitolite. While it is not suitable in sites where strict control and auditability are required, it is very useful in most other sites, not only saving the administrator a lot of time, but the users also do not have to wait on the administrator for something they need quickly.

In the next chapter, we will talk about what **core** Gitolite is and what **non-core is**, look at some non-core programs that come with Gitolite, and discuss customizing Gitolite by adding our own non-core code.

9
Customizing Gitolite

It must be clear by this time that Gitolite is a pretty powerful tool for managing Git repositories on a server. The most powerful tools, however, allow the administrator to add features that are unique to their site, and thus cannot be expected to be added to the product itself. For example, consider Git itself, its *hooks* mechanism (see `man githooks` for details) contains several predefined hooks, which the user can install on their repositories to customize Git's behavior at various points in the lifecycle of a commit, a rebase, a push, and so on. In fact, Gitolite's ability to perform branch level access control (as opposed to merely repository level access control) is *entirely* done by using Git's `update` hook.

Core and non-core Gitolite

Gitolite goes a little further than merely allowing you to customize it for your location-specific needs. Gitolite actually *ships* with customizations already in place for several optional features. Some of these customizations are enabled by default, while others are disabled, though requiring only a quick edit of `$HOME/.gitolite.rc` to enable them.

As a result, Gitolite makes a distinction between **core** and **non-core** Gitolite code. If you happened to look into the Gitolite source tree (under `src` if you cloned the Gitolite source code), you will notice several directories at the top level, and a couple of files. Of these, gitolite considers the following directories to contain non-core code: `commands`, `syntactic-sugar`, `triggers`, `lib/Gitolite/Triggers`, and `VREF`. Everything else is considered *core*.

Making this distinction also helps in deciding whether a new feature is to be added or not. If the feature requires change to core Gitolite, a lot more careful consideration and thought will go into it, and even then it will only happen if the change is really needed by several users. In practice, however, Gitolite's customization feature is so powerful that it has become increasingly rare that any change to core Gitolite is required.

Types of non-core code and examples

Gitolite allows four types of customizations you can develop for your site. This might sound somewhat intimidating, but in practice most people use only two of them. We'll describe each of them now.

Commands

Gitolite allows remote users to run some specific commands on the server, in the form `ssh git@host command-name`. Commands need to be enabled before they can be used remotely; see the section on making changes to the `rc` file in *Chapter 8, Allowing Users to Create Repos*. One way to look at this is to view it as giving users a very restricted shell to use, which allows only specific commands to be executed.

We've already encountered some Gitolite commands, the `perms` and `D` commands in *Chapter 8, Allowing Users to Create Repos*, for instance, and `info` and `help` in earlier chapters. Gitolite ships with more than twenty commands, although only five are enabled for remote use by default. A few more are listed in `$HOME/.gitolite.rc`, but left disabled by being commented out. It only takes a removal of the comment marker in the line to enable them.

Many of the commands that Gitolite comes with, however, are not meant for remote use at all and thus, they are not listed (even in commented out form) in `$HOME/.gitolite.rc`. These commands are meant as helpers to server-side scripts or other non-core programs. One of the most convenient of these is the `access` command, which has the following help message:

```
Usage:  gitolite access [-q] <repo> <user> <perm> <ref>


Print access rights for arguments given.  The string printed has the word
DENIED in it if access was denied.  With '-q', returns only an exit code
(shell truth, not perl truth -- 0 is success).


    - repo: mandatory
    - user: mandatory
    - perm: defauts to '+'.  Valid values: R, W, +, C, D, M
    - ref:  defaults to 'any'.  See notes below

Notes:
    - ref: Any fully qualified ref ('refs/heads/master', not 'master') is
fine.
```

```
    The 'any' ref is special -- it ignores deny rules (see docs for what
this

    means and exceptions).


Batch mode: see src/triggers/post-compile/update-git-daemon-access-list
for a

good example that shows how to test several repos in one invocation.
This is

orders of magnitude faster than running the command multiple times;
you'll

notice if you have more than a hundred or so repos.
```

As you can see, this is of great use in rolling your own code, where you would like to check a user's access rights to a repository or several repositories.

Running `gitolite help` on the server will list all available commands; just as running `ssh git@host help` will list all commands available *remotely*. In addition, Gitolite comes with several commands that are implemented internally in Gitolite. They are, in effect, part of the "core". Run `gitolite -h` to get a list of them with brief descriptions.

All Gitolite commands respond with a usage message when invoked with a single argument of `-h`. If you write your own commands, it would be a good idea to adhere to this convention.

Here's a list of some of the existing commands in Gitolite with a brief description of each:

- `access`: This prints or tests access rights on a repository for a user. This is useful when you write your own commands. See the description of the `fork` command below for one example.

- `D`: This lets a user delete a repository that they created (see *Chapter 8, Allowing Users to Create Repos*).

- `desc`: This shows or sets a description for a user-created repository.

- `fork`: This forks a repo on the server. This takes a repository and creates a new one with the same content. It checks to make sure the reader has read access to the source repository, and is allowed to create the destination repository (see *Chapter 8, Allowing Users to Create Repos*). This command uses the `-l` option to `git clone`, so it runs really fast. (Without this command, the alternative would be for the user to clone the source repository, and then use that to create and push to the destination repository. For large repositories, this could take a while).

- `git-config`: This prints (or tests existence of) 'config' values in the repo.
- `help`: This prints a list of all the available commands.
- `info`: This prints your username, the git/gitolite version numbers, and any repositories you have access to.
- `perms`: This lists or sets permissions for a user-created repository.

In a subsequent section, we will see how to create your own commands.

Syntactic sugar

Syntactic sugar scripts are a form of customization that most people will rarely, if ever, have to write, or even encounter. They are useful for situations where the administrator would like some additional, purely syntax-related feature added to Gitolite's access control language. In such situations, a syntactic sugar helper script can be written that changes what the administrator writes into something Gitolite can parse.

Gitolite ships with a few syntactic sugar helper scripts. For example, one is to allow C-style continuation lines in Gitolite's conf file, since normally Gitolite does not allow that. Another is to provide a simple macro facility.

Triggers

Arguably, the most powerful of Gitolite's customization features is the trigger feature. Gitolite triggers are the equivalent of Git's hooks. Just as Git provides hooks that run at various points (for example, pre-commit, pre-receive, and post-receive, to name a few), similarly Gitolite's triggers also run at specific points in the lifecycle of a Gitolite managed push or fetch.

There is a difference between Git hooks and Gitolite trigger programs though. Git defines several hooks and requires that your hook code be named exactly one of those (for example, post-receive or update). Gitolite on the other hand allows you to define a list of trigger programs, which it will invoke in sequence when the trigger point is reached. It is only the name of the trigger point that is fixed. This also means, of course, that your programs can be called whatever you like.

The important trigger points, from a customization point of view, are INPUT, POST_CREATE, and POST_COMPILE, although there are several other trigger points supported.

The purpose of an INPUT trigger is to manipulate the input arguments or the environment in some way. Since a child program cannot affect the parent's environment, INPUT triggers need to be written in Perl and installed as modules in lib/Gitolite/Triggers (as opposed to being plain programs in any language, that are installed in the triggers directory). Examples of features using the INPUT trigger are giving some users full shell access and allowing repositories to have aliases.

 This chapter will contain references to many non-core features that are out of scope for this book. Please refer to Gitolite's online documentation for details.

The POST_CREATE trigger point is useful to run any housekeeping or reporting tasks that need to be performed after a new repository is created. For example, Gitolite uses this trigger point to run code that updates the access lists for gitweb and git-daemon whenever a user creates a *wild* repository.

The POST_COMPILE trigger point helps you perform additional tasks when the gitolite-admin repository is pushed. This trigger point is associated with the maximum number of programs shipped with Gitolite. Most of them have to do with with ssh keys, or updating access lists for gitweb and git-daemon.

Virtual refs

The final type of non-core customization available is Gitolite's ability to make access decisions based on what Gitolite calls virtual refs. The scripts that do this are called VREFs; they are complex and important enough to have the next chapter be devoted entirely to them.

Writing your own non-core code

It's reasonably easy to write your own code to add features that are specific to your site. For example, suppose we want an e-mail to be sent to the administrator every time a developer creates a *wild repository*. We will assume that the standard Unix utilities exist and are available. In particular, we will assume the Unix mail command is available. This command takes the message from standard input, and the subject and recipient data from command-line arguments, and sends the e-mail, thus suits our purposes very well.

Since this is an action that needs to run when a repository is created, it needs to be added to the POST_CREATE trigger list. According to the Gitolite documentation, when a wild repository is created, each program in the POST_CREATE trigger list is called with the second argument being the name of the repository that was just created, while the third argument is the name of the user who created it. (If this is empty, this is not a wild repository creation but a normal repository creation; that is, by the administrator adding the repository to the Gitolite conf file and pushing the change.)

As a result, this code could be as simple as follows:

```
#!/bin/bash
[ -n $3 ] && echo | mail -s "new repo $2 created" admin_group@example.com
```

Now we've written this code, we need to put it somewhere that Gitolite will find it and use it at the right time.

We decide to create a new directory called $HOME/local to hold all our local customizations. In this directory, we add a subdirectory called triggers, and into this we place this script, naming it new-repo-alert. (Don't forget to chmod +x the script!)

Now, we edit Gitolite's rc file ($HOME/.gitolite.rc). In this file, we find a line that defines the LOCAL_CODE variable commented out but conveniently pointing to precisely where we chose to place our customizations, so we simply uncomment it.

We then add the following lines of code immediately after the LOCAL_CODE variable:

```
POST_CREATE => [
    'new-repo-alert',
],
```

Did you note the trailing comma after the closing bracket? And that's really all you need to do. From now on, any time a user creates a new "wild" repository; the new-repo-alert script will be executed.

As a second example, we will create a small command. The example we use will allow a user to check the size of a repository using the git count-objects command. Our command will default to running it with the -v option because that is the most generic and useful.

To do that, create a directory called $HOME/local/commands, and put a script called count-objects in that directory. Make sure the script is executable (chmod +x). The code for the script is as follows:

```bash
#!/bin/bash

repo=$1

gitolite access -q $repo $GL_USER W any || {
    echo Sorry $GL_USER, you are not authorized
    exit 1
}


cd $GL_REPO_BASE/$repo.git
git count-objects -v
```

The interesting part of this code is not the actual count-objects command. The most generic, and thus most usable for your needs, is the gitolite access command, whose usage message we have already seen in an earlier section. Here, we are using it to ensure that the user running the command has at least got write access to the repository in question before allowing the command to run.

Finally, add this command to the list of commands in rc file's ENABLE list, preferably in the COMMANDS section.

Note that count-objects is a harmless command, so it may not need to be protected. However, if you then stretch the use case a little and allow the user to start a git gc operation, or even a git fsck, you need to be more careful. Some of those commands don't deal well with being run too many times or simultaneously by multiple people. Ensure your command does some rate limiting or serializing.

Other commands require arguments to be supplied. If your script takes arguments from the user, be sure to sanitize them before running the command. You can undermine all of Gitolite's access control with one carelessly written command!

As you can see from these two examples, the most important aspect of adding a new feature to your site is to decide when and how the feature should be invoked—should it be a user command, or a trigger that runs at specific points, or perhaps a VREF that can influence the outcome of the overall command, and so on. In some cases, it could even be a combination, for instance, a command and a VREF working together. As an extreme example, Gitolite's mirroring feature, which is written entirely as non-core code, is implemented as one command, and one Perl module is added to each of the INPUT, PRE_GIT, and POST_GIT trigger lists.

Summary

In this chapter, we have seen an introduction to how Gitolite can be customized or new features can be added that are specific to your site. This is a fairly complex topic, but if you get your hands dirty and start writing programs, you will soon get very comfortable with the idea, as well as get a very good feel for how powerful the feature actually is.

The next chapter will focus on VREF, a powerful feature for even more fine-grained access control, as well as access control based on factors other than what Gitolite normally uses.

10
Understanding VREFs

We looked at VREFs briefly in *Chapter 7, Advanced Access Control and Configuration,* including a small example to illustrate how Gitolite can allow or reject pushes based on which files have been modified in commits being pushed. In this chapter, we will explore VREFs in much greater detail, since this is one of the most powerful features of Gitolite. We will start small, describing the simplest use for VREFs, then move on to more complex uses.

Migrating update hooks

Some sites may already have been using update hooks in their existing (pre-Gitolite) repository setups. Since Gitolite reserves the update hook for itself, this presents a bit of a problem in terms of switching over.

If your site has such update hooks, the VREF mechanism can help replace them. Replacing update hooks is one of the simplest uses of VREFs, but understanding how that is done is also a good first step to understanding the full power of Gitolite's VREF mechanism.

To convert your existing update hooks to VREFs, you first create a directory called VREF within `$HOME/local` (we're continuing the convention from *Chapter 9, Customizing Gitolite,* that the `LOCAL_CODE` variable in the `rc` file points here). Then, copy each unique update hook into this newly created directory, renaming each update hook in some way.

As an example, say you had one repository that was frequently worked on by novice users using Windows, and so the update hook was used to make sure there were no line-ending problems. You might rename this to `check-crlf`.

Now, for each repository that needs this check to be made (that is, each repository that had used that specific update hook in the pre-Gitolite setup), add a rule like this:

```
-   VREF/check-crlf  =  @all
```

When Gitolite's update hook is processing a push, it will encounter this VREF rule and it will call the `check-crlf` program. The first three arguments passed are the same that Git itself has passed to the update hook, and if the program exits with a non-zero exit code, Gitolite will reject the push. No changes to the `check-crlf` code are needed to make all this happen; it just works.

Astute readers will have noticed that they could, instead of the rule shown above, use:

```
-   VREF/check-crlf  =  @junior-developers
```

This helps to limit the checking to only those users named in the rule. *In other words, Gitolite allows a plain old update hook to be selectively applied*, which could be very useful.

Passing arguments to the VREF code

Now let us suppose we had an update hook (in our pre-Gitolite setup) that prevented certain users from making changes to certain files. One way would be to write an update hook that checks for such files and use it as a VREF, as shown in the previous section. However, the list or pattern of files to be checked will need to somehow be encoded within the VREF code, or some other method of passing that information needs to be found.

Gitolite allows you to pass additional arguments to the VREF code. Let's say the VREF used is called NAME, then instead of merely saying:

```
-   VREF/NAME             =  @junior-developers
```

and making sure that the code for the NAME VREF knows which files we are talking about, you can say:

```
-   VREF/NAME/.*\.h$      =  @junior-developers
```

You'll see how this becomes really useful if you later find that another group of users needs to be restricted in a similar way, but for a different set of files. Let's say we have a set of technical writers who are working on the documentation; there's no reason for them to be touching the files that make up the source code:

```
-   VREF/NAME/.*\.[ch]$   =  @tech-writers
```

Of course, the VREF code is now not quite the same as it was when it was an update hook. Apart from the first three arguments (which are the same as those listed in man githooks for the `update` hook), there are now several other arguments, and the file patterns we just added are one of those (specifically, the eighth argument). The VREF code must get that pattern out of the incoming arguments and use it to decide whether the push is to be allowed or denied.

Using the permission field

Let us say we have several different kinds of source code files, and listing all of them in the rule for the technical writer is not only cumbersome, but error prone because we might miss something. We do know, however, that technical writers only work on documents, so we'd prefer to simply restrict them to `*.odt` files.

Until now, we have considered the NAME VREF to behave in a certain way: receive a filename pattern, and if any file has been changed (in the push) that matches that pattern, exit with a non-zero return code to signal Gitolite to reject the push. As you can see, this behavior completely ignores the permission field; that is, even this rule would have the same effect:

```
RW+     VREF/NAME/.*\.[ch]$  =  @tech-writers
```

What we need is a way to consider the permission field as well. Our first impulse might be to develop some way to pass this field to the VREF code, perhaps with some new syntax, and let the VREF code reverse the check when required.

However, this complicates the VREF code, while at the same time not making use of Gitolite's rule processing logic.

Gitolite processes access control rules based on matching a *ref* (typically something like refs/heads/master or refs/tags/v1.0) against each rule in turn. So one way to make use of this is to not have the VREF code actually make a decision, but merely *output something* that Gitolite can capture and run through its access control rules, just like a normal *ref* would be.

You could call this a *virtual ref*, too!

Let us briefly recap the terminology, a VREF is the code that runs, and a virtual ref is what it might send back to Gitolite.

Maintaining the update hook function

However, we do not want to affect the behavior of a standard (Git) update hook when used as a VREF, as described earlier in this chapter. This is easy enough—Gitolite treats any lines in the VREF's output as virtual refs only if they start with VREF/, and even that only if the VREF has exited with zero status.

Default is success

At this point we need to change the NAME VREF. Instead of making a decision, it should merely print all the files that have been changed, each prefixed with VREF/NAME/.

Once that is done, it might then seem that the following rule is all we need:

```
RW+     VREF/NAME/.*\.odt$  =  @tech-writers
```

However, that's not quite the end of it.

There's a slight difference in how virtual refs are treated compared to real refs. With real refs, if no access rule matches the ref (and the user, and the actual type of write), the default is to reject the push.

However, virtual refs are designed as *additional* rules, adding checks that the normal Gitolite access rules cannot. Thus it makes more sense that if no VREFs match, it should be as if no additional checks *apply* to this push, and so the default is to *allow* the push.

As a result, we need one more rule, which brings our final ruleset to this:

```
RW+     VREF/NAME/.*\.odt$  =  @tech-writers
-       VREF/NAME/          =  @tech-writers
```

Loosely speaking, what this does is, for each file that has been changed, generate a virtual ref by prefixing VREF/NAME/ to it, and passing that virtual ref through the ruleset. The rest is obvious, for example, changing a file called foo.c creates a virtual ref called VREF/NAME/foo.c, which will match only the second rule and this push gets denied. Files whose names end in .odt will match the first rule and not cause a reject.

Example VREFs and their usage

The Gitolite source tree comes with a few VREFs ready to be used. To use them, you simply add rules similar to the ones we saw at the end of the previous section. We will look at a couple of them to get a feel for how they are used, and then design one from scratch so we know how to add our own.

 If you look in the Gitolite source tree, you won't actually find a VREF called NAME. This is because NAME is special and the code for that is built in to Gitolite.

Newcomers to Git may sometimes end up creating a commit that changes a lot more files than are strictly necessary for the change being made. Perhaps they added debugging statements to some other files, or perhaps they accidentally saved some files with a different line-ending (Unix LF versus Windows CRLF), and so on.

If you are sure that your new developers are given relatively simple tasks, and at no time should any particular task touch more than, say, five files, you can use the COUNT VREF to prevent them from pushing more, and thus protect the repository from wide-ranging changes of the kind discussed in the previous paragraph. Here's a rule that achieves that:

```
-    VREF/COUNT/5    =    @new-devs
```

The COUNT VREF essentially counts all the files changed in the commits that constitute the current push (and do not exist on any other branch or tag).

If that last bit sounds complicated, consider what happens when a developer merely makes a new branch out of an existing one and pushes it. We don't want the COUNT VREF to basically see all the files in the branch as changed, simply because the old value of the branch pushed was empty. This is why the COUNT code looks at commits that do not appear in any other ref.

The MAX_NEWBIN_SIZE VREF is similar in concept. This addresses the issue that sometimes developers unintentionally or unknowingly commit, say, a JAR file or the executable file produced by a build step. Executable files like this tend to be a bit larger than normal source files, so if you have some idea of a reasonable limit, you can use this VREF to enforce it.

Writing your own VREF

Here's an example use case where VREFs come in handy. We'll use this to design a very simple VREF, in a way that cannot be done with the existing rules.

The requirement is simple: for any repository `foo`, if a repository called `l10n` contains a directory called `foo`, then you cannot push any files called `*.po` to `foo`.

> This has been adapted from a more complex, real-life use case, but for our purposes we don't need more than this. As you might guess, this is a multi-repository system that is gradually moving toward centralizing the local language files so that translators only have to deal with one repository. Each repository's local language files are moved over when they are deemed ready and from that point on, localization files must go to the single repository that was created for the purpose.

Because this is a very specific use case, we can write a simple VREF that does not take any arguments. Our rule can look like this:

```
repo @all
-   VREF/l10n-check  =  @all
```

As you can see, we're applying this rule to all repositories. (This is slightly inefficient if you have several repositories for which this will never be true—the VREF will be invoked for each of them, on every push. If so, replace `@all` in the `repo` line with a group name that contains only those repositories for which this check is required)

> There may be individual rules for each of those repositories elsewhere—we need not put this VREF rule in each repository section. This is an example of the *Rule Accumulation and Delegation*, discussed in *Chapter 6, Getting Started with Access Control* in action.

Here's one way to code this VREF (some familiarity with basic shell syntax and Git concepts is required to understand this code):

```
#!/bin/bash


# see Gitolite documentation for arguments and meanings
oldtree=$4
```

```
newtree=$5
refex=$7


# no *.po files changed?  No problem!
git diff --name-only $oldtree $newtree | grep '.*\.po$' >/dev/null ||
exit 0


cd $GL_REPO_BASE/l10n.git
# no directory with the same name as $GL_REPO in the l10n repo?  No
problem!
git ls-tree master | grep "\s$GL_REPO$" >/dev/null || exit 0


echo $refex "sorry, PO files must be added to '$GL_REPO' subdirectory in
'l10n' repo"
```

As you can see, the first check uses the git diff command to check whether this push has changed any po files. If not, there's nothing to check and we exit without doing anything. The second check moves to the l10n repository, then runs an ls-tree on that repository to check whether it contains a file or directory whose name is the same as the repository that the user is pushing. If it does not, we can exit without complaint.

If those two checks succeed, we need to signal the error. One way would be to simply exit 1; Gitolite would catch the VREF code dying and reject the push. On the other hand, we could print the refex itself (which in this case is just VREF/l10n, but it's a good habit to use the argument instead). It will then match the access rule we set up, and because the permission is "-", the push will be rejected.

But the VREF feature offers a little more. If, after the refex, you print a space and then some explanatory message, this message will be printed when the push is rejected:

```
$ git push
Counting objects: 4, done.
Delta compression using up to 4 threads.
Compressing objects: 100% (2/2), done.
Writing objects: 100% (3/3), 351 bytes | 0 bytes/s, done.
Total 3 (delta 0), reused 0 (delta 0)
remote: FATAL: W VREF/l10n t2 u1 DENIED by VREF/l10n
```

```
remote: sorry, PO files must be added to 't2' subdirectory in 'l10n' repo
remote:
remote: error: hook declined to update refs/heads/master
To u1:t2
 ! [remote rejected] master -> master (hook declined)
error: failed to push some refs to 'u1:t2'
```

If you write VREFs to catch rarely occurring conditions, then you may find it useful to augment Gitolite's rather spartan error reporting with something in plain English, so your users can scratch their heads a little less!

Summary

In this chapter, we explored one of Gitolite's most powerful features—the ability to use arbitrary external factors for access control decisions by writing VREFs. The next chapter will conclude our exploration of Gitolite by talking about mirroring—a feature which large multi-site setups could find very useful.

11
Mirroring

While most installations are happy to install Gitolite on a single server accessible to all their developers, some of them have developers in several cities around the world, and it is often useful to provide local mirrors in each city for fast access. Gitolite's mirroring feature caters to these needs in a very flexible manner.

Mirroring can be as simple or as complex as you want it. You can have one server be the master server for all repositories, with one or more slave servers carrying copies of them. You can have different servers be the master servers for different repositories, and select only some of the remaining servers as slaves instead of all of them. You can even keep some repositories out of the mirroring process if you wish.

Terminology and basic concepts

A mirrored repository has a writable copy on one server, often called the **master server** for that repository, and read-only copies on one or more servers, similarly called **slave servers**. The slave repositories are updated near instantaneously, subject to network speed, when the master repository is updated.

Repository level mirroring

The primary purpose of most mirroring is to make read access (over the network) faster, by providing a copy on a nearby server for fetches and clones. One might, therefore, expect a single server to be designated as the master and several others as slave servers.

However, Gitolite mirroring is defined at the *repository* level, not for the entire server as a whole. For *each* repository, the administrator decides which server holds the master (writable) copy, and which of the other servers, if any, should make slave copies available to their local users. (This is why we speak of master repository and slave repository, not master server and slave server.)

This is a very important idea that brings several advantages over mirroring the entire server as a whole.

Firstly, repositories need not be made available on servers where there are no local users of that repository. If there are very few (say one or two) users, depending on how actively developed the repository is, it might still make sense, from a network utilization point of view, to let those few users directly pull from the master or one of the other slaves. This allows branch offices with less resources to still be part of the Gitolite mirroring network if they have enough projects their local users will be working on.

Secondly, since you do not have to put *all* the master repositories on the same server, you can choose where to place the master copy of any specific repository. Usually, you'll want to place it on whichever server is closest (from a network speed point of view) to the majority of the developers who will be working on it.

Finally, repositories can be purely local to a particular server, that is, they need not be mirrored at all.

 There can only be one master repository — you cannot have different users pushing to different servers because that would lead to a merge issue, which cannot be reliably automated. (However, Gitolite does have a workaround for convenience, as we will see later.)

The gitolite-admin repository

From the point of view of Gitolite's mirroring feature, the gitolite-admin repository is just another repository. There is nothing special about it as far as mirroring is concerned – like all other repositories, one of the servers will hold the master (writable) copy. The only difference is that *all* the other servers must be mentioned in the slave list; if a server is not mentioned, it cannot receive updates to this repository.

Setting up mirroring

Setting up mirroring has quite a few manual steps, although each step in itself is quite simple. The first step is to give each host a name, and make sure that the hosts can all talk to one another by these names. The second step is to enable mirroring on each server.

We start by installing Gitolite as normal on all the servers. Then, we edit each server's `$HOME/.gitolite.rc` file and uncomment the line defining the HOSTNAME, choosing a simple hostname as the value.

The hostname should be a simple word; it is of interest only to Gitolite and does not have any relation to the server's hostname as known by the operating system and DNS records.

Gitolite mirroring works by allowing the servers to communicate with each other using ssh keypairs named after these hostnames. This is the same mechanism that users use, except that the public key file for a server is named `server-`, followed by the hostname of that server. All the keys will need to be provided to all the servers, added to their gitolite-admin repositories, and pushed. Finally, each server's $HOME/.ssh/config will need a host alias to refer to all the other machines.

Example setup

An example will make this clearer. Say you have three servers jupiter, ganymede, and callisto. These servers are on IP addresses `10.1.1.1`, `10.2.1.1` and `10.3.1.1`.

1. First, install Gitolite on all three servers. On Jupiter, edit `$HOME/.gitolite.rc`, and uncomment the `HOSTNAME` line, changing it as follows (don't miss the trailing comma!):

    ```
    HOSTNAME    => "jupiter",
    ```

2. Do the same on the other two servers.

3. Run `ssh-keygen` on each server to create a key pair for the server. Collect all three `$HOME/.ssh/id_rsa.pub` files (one from each server), naming them `server-jupiter.pub`, `server-callisto.pub`, and `server-ganymede.pub` respectively.

4. Add these public keys to *all* the servers, just as you would add normal users (that is, *for each server*, clone the gitolite-admin repo from that server, add all these keys to the `keydir`, then add, commit, and push).

5. Next, add the following lines to all three servers' `$HOME/.ssh/config` files (assuming the hosting user on all three servers is `git`):

    ```
    host jupiter
        user git
        hostname 10.1.1.1
    host ganymede
        user git
        hostname 10.2.1.1
    host callisto
        user git
        hostname 10.3.1.1
    ```

When you're done with all this, you should be able to test your setup by running ssh ganymede info from jupiter. You should get an output similar to the following:

```
hello server-jupiter, this is git@ganymede.example.com running gitolite3
v3.5.3.1-7-g31d11b9 on git 1.8.3.1
```

Similar commands from any server to any other should generate similar responses. It is best to test all the possible combinations to avoid confusing errors later.

Bootstrapping the mirroring process

The previous step establishes communication and authentication between all servers. Once that is done and checked, the next step is to bootstrap the mirroring process by setting up mirror options for the gitolite-admin repository and pushing them.

On each server, add the following lines to the conf file:

```
repo gitolite-admin
    option mirror.master    = jupiter
    option mirror.slaves    = callisto ganymede
```

Once you add, commit, and push this change to all the repositories, Gitolite mirroring is set up and ready to go. From here on, you administer everything by pushing to the gitolite-admin repository on its master server (in our case, jupiter).

Mirroring other repositories

By now you can guess what you need to do for each of the other repositories. Just add option lines as in the previous section for each of them. For example, a simple mirroring setup, where all the repositories are mirrored the same way, can be as follows:

```
repo @all
    option mirror.master    = jupiter
    option mirror.slaves    = callisto ganymede
```

If that's all you want, you're pretty much done with mirroring. Otherwise, add the options as required, giving each repository the correct master server name and the correct set of slave servers. Note that any repositories that don't have these settings are considered local.

If you're allowing your users to create their own repositories (see *Chapter 8, Allowing Users to Create Repos*), just add mirroring option lines to those repository definitions too. The following restrictions apply to mirroring user-created repositories.

The creation of such a repository is propagated only when the first push happens to the repository on the master server. A repository created as the result of a clone or fetch will not immediately propagate to the slaves.

Changes in permissions (using the `perms` command; see *Chapter 8, Allowing Users to Create Repos*, specifically the *Giving access to other users* section) also propagate only on the next push.

Local repositories and hostname substitution

We mentioned earlier that some servers can have local repositories, say if the `conf` file does not specify Gitolite mirror options for those repositories. However, local repositories are really of interest only if each server can have its own set of them. For example, say the folks on Ganymede wish to have a local repository called ganymede-news that they intend to use internally. Adding that to the `conf` file would create such a repository on Jupiter and Callisto as well; even if no one used it, it's ugly, unnecessary, and cause for future confusion. We would like to prevent this, but since the same gitolite-admin repository, with the same `conf/gitolite.conf` file and other files, is pushed to all the slave servers, it seems difficult to do so.

The feature that makes this possible is HOSTNAME substitution. Specifically, whenever Gitolite encounters the string %HOSTNAME (followed by a non-word character; that is, a character other than alphabets, digits, and underscore) in the `conf` file, it will replace it with the HOSTNAME of the server, as given in `$HOME/.gitolite.rc`, before processing it.

Using the `include` statement capability we saw in *Chapter 6, Getting Started with Access Control*, you can now provide server-specific Gitolite configuration, while still keeping everything in one repository. Just add the following line to the main conf file (`conf/gitolite.conf`):

```
include "%HOSTNAME.conf"
```

Then, create `conf/jupiter.conf`, `conf/callisto.conf` and so on for each of your servers. Within those files, specify repo statements and rules that are unique to the respective server.

It is important to understand that when you use such an `include` statement in your main `conf` file and push, each server will see that line differently. For example, Jupiter will see it as the following line (and similarly for other servers):

```
include "jupiter.conf"
```

This means that the other two files (`ganymede.conf` and `callisto.conf`), while they are certainly physically present in the `conf` directory, are not actually processed at all.

Redirecting pushes

We mentioned earlier that there can only be one master repository. However, this makes things a little inconvenient from the developers' point of view. Say you would like some of your developers to take advantage of a geographically close slave server to pull updates from. This means they would have to use push to a different server than the one they presumably cloned from and regularly pull/fetch from. While Git does allow this (see man git-config and look for pushurl, for one possible way), it is still something that requires each user to do something on their machines. In addition, remember Gitolite allows different repositories to have different master servers; this is more scope for confusion on the part of the developer.

Therefore, Gitolite has a feature that makes this restriction much less onerous. If the administrator chooses, a developer can push to a slave server, and *the push will transparently be forwarded to the master server for that repository*. In fact, the user may not even know that this is happening unless the network speed makes it obvious.

This makes things very convenient for administrators; there is no longer any need to confuse developers with detailed information about where to clone and where to push for each repository they need. In fact, you can set it up so that all developers in a particular site use their local Gitolite server for all their clones, without even having to even know that Gitolite mirroring is being used!

This feature is called **redirected push**, since that is exactly what happens behind the scenes. Here's how to use it. Let us say you want to allow redirected pushes (to a `repository foo`) from `ganymede` (but not `callisto`), you add the following lines to the `conf` file:

```
repo foo
    option mirror.redirectOK  = ganymede
```

That's it. Just list all the slaves that you trust and add them, space-separated, as a value to this option. If you trust all of them, just use the single word all instead.

Manual synchronization

Sometimes you will find that a slave server has not been updated, perhaps due to some transient network problem. One way to get it back in sync, after the network problem has been resolved, of course, is to make some change to the repository and make a push. However, this feels clumsy and inelegant.

 At present, Gitolite does not have any way of reporting on push failures, although it does log whatever messages Git itself sends back in the log files. This means admins have to actively monitor the log files for failure, or wait for users to report issues with slaves getting out of sync.

For the aesthetically sensitive, Gitolite has the mirror command. Just log on to the server that contains the master repository, and run `gitolite mirror push slavename reponame`. This will immediately bring the slave up to date.

If you would like remote users to invoke such updates, simply enable the command for remote use by uncommenting the corresponding line in `$HOME/.gitolite.rc`.

Switching to a different master

The biggest day-to-day benefit of mirroring is clearly that it can make read access more network-efficient for projects where the development team is widely distributed, albeit at the cost of an extra server at each slave location.

However, there's obviously one more advantage. If the main server for a repository should fail, one of the mirrors can easily be removed from the list of slaves and be made the master. As long as there are no network problems, the slave should be in the same state as the master, so no commits are lost.

 Mirroring is not the same as backup. It is outside the scope of this book to discuss the differences, but you should always have a reliable backup system in place for all your servers and possible workstations as well.

This simple strategy breaks down when the server that died contains the gitolite-admin repository itself. This is a bit of a catch-22 situation; you cannot push the change (in mirror options for the gitolite-admin repository) to the current master server since it is down. Yet, you cannot push to the slave server that you decided to promote to "master" status, because it does not yet know that it is the new master! (Needless to say, as a security feature, slave servers do not accept pushes from just anywhere – they will only do so from the server that they have been told is the master for the repository concerned.)

The correct way to resolve this is as follows:

1. On each slave, edit `$HOME/.gitolite/gitolite.conf`. Change the master and slave options for the gitolite-admin repository. If you used repo `@all` for these options, they will change for everyone. However, it's best to change it only for the gitolite-admin repository if at all possible.

2. After saving the change to this file, run `gitolite setup`. This will override the restriction and force the change on the local server. (This cannot be done remotely, again for security reasons.)

3. Now, on the administrator's workstation, clone the gitolite-admin repository from the new master, change the mirroring options for the rest of the repositories (if required), then push the change.

Summary

This concludes our exploration of Gitolite's mirroring feature. While it is not something that everyone will need, for the larger sites this has some very visible benefits.

I hope you have enjoyed this exploration of Gitolite and its features. As you use Gitolite more and more, you might also have the need to look at the official documentation on `http://gitolite.com`. We hope that this book has helped you understand the concepts and rationale behind Gitolite so that you can understand the official documentation better and get your job done faster.

Index

Thank you for buying
Gitolite Essentials

About Packt Publishing

Packt, pronounced 'packed', published its first book "*Mastering phpMyAdmin for Effective MySQL Management*" in April 2004 and subsequently continued to specialize in publishing highly focused books on specific technologies and solutions.

Our books and publications share the experiences of your fellow IT professionals in adapting and customizing today's systems, applications, and frameworks. Our solution based books give you the knowledge and power to customize the software and technologies you're using to get the job done. Packt books are more specific and less general than the IT books you have seen in the past. Our unique business model allows us to bring you more focused information, giving you more of what you need to know, and less of what you don't.

Packt is a modern, yet unique publishing company, which focuses on producing quality, cutting-edge books for communities of developers, administrators, and newbies alike. For more information, please visit our website: www.packtpub.com.

About Packt Open Source

In 2010, Packt launched two new brands, Packt Open Source and Packt Enterprise, in order to continue its focus on specialization. This book is part of the Packt Open Source brand, home to books published on software built around Open Source licences, and offering information to anybody from advanced developers to budding web designers. The Open Source brand also runs Packt's Open Source Royalty Scheme, by which Packt gives a royalty to each Open Source project about whose software a book is sold.

Writing for Packt

We welcome all inquiries from people who are interested in authoring. Book proposals should be sent to author@packtpub.com. If your book idea is still at an early stage and you would like to discuss it first before writing a formal book proposal, contact us; one of our commissioning editors will get in touch with you.

We're not just looking for published authors; if you have strong technical skills but no writing experience, our experienced editors can help you develop a writing career, or simply get some additional reward for your expertise.

GitLab Repository Management

ISBN: 978-1-78328-179-4   Paperback: 88 pages

Delve into managing your projects with GitLab, while tailoring it to fit your environment

1. Understand how to efficiently track and manage projects.

2. Establish teams with a fast software developing tool.

3. Employ teams constructively in a GitLab environment.

Git: Version Control for Everyone

ISBN: 978-1-84951-752-2   Paperback: 180 pages

The non-coder's guide to everyday version control for increased efficiency and productivity

1. A complete beginner's workflow for version control of common documents and content.

2. Examples used are from non-techie, day to day computing activities we all engage in.

3. Learn through multiple modes – readers learn theory to understand the concept and reinforce it by practical tutorials.

4. Ideal for users on Windows, Linux, and Mac OS X.

Please check **www.PacktPub.com** for information on our titles

PUBLISHING

Instant RubyMine Assimilation

ISBN: 978-1-84969-876-4   Paperback: 66 pages

Utilize the RubyMine IDE to develop your own Ruby on Rails applications

1. Learn something new in an Instant! A short, fast, focused guide delivering immediate results.

2. Incorporate features of RubyMine into your everyday Ruby and Ruby on Rails development workflow.

3. Learn about the integrated testing and debugging tools to make your coding bulletproof and productive.

4. Become an expert at deploying Rails applications directly from RubyMine.

Cloning Internet Applications with Ruby

ISBN: 978-1-84951-106-3   Paperback: 336 pages

Make your own TinyURL, Twitter, Flickr, or Facebook using Ruby

1. Build your own custom social networking, URL shortening, and photo sharing websites using Ruby.

2. Deploy and launch your custom high-end web applications.

3. Learn what makes popular social networking sites such as Twitter and Facebook tick.

4. Understand features of some of the most famous photo sharing and social networking websites.

Please check **www.PacktPub.com** for information on our titles

CPSIA information can be obtained at www.ICGtesting.com
Printed in the USA
LVOW03s0042160914

404165LV00008B/85/P

9 781783 282371